When the Mountains Call You

by

Lisa Malawski

RoseDog Books
PITTSBURGH, PENNSYLVANIA 15238

RoseDog Books
585 Alpha Drive, Suite 103
Pittsburgh, PA 15238
Visit our website at *www.rosedogbookstore.com*

ISBN: 979-8-88812-337-9
eISBN: 979-8-88812-837-4

This book is part of a series

The title of this book is a metaphor for when middle-age calls you, when empty nest syndrome calls you, when menopause calls you, when death calls you, when love calls you, when rescuing a dog calls you, when relocating to another state calls you, when fixing your mental health calls you, and when racial disparity calls you.

What will you do? How will you respond?

Acknowledgements

The author would like to thank the readers for their lust of reading and for the internal powers that they possess which they can use to make changes in their own lives or in the lives of characters that are outside of this book.

The author would like to express her gratitude to Scott for his love and support.

Additionally, the author would like to thank Scott and Ronnie for their editing expertise and patience.

All of my love to Anthony and Sheba for being a constant presence in my life.

Table of Contents

Take the Masks Off!

Hope is laying in her daughter's empty room. She is thinking of when she was young, over twenty-five years ago and she had her house in Florida. She remembers the masks she had on the wall. The masks were different colors, white, black, and brown with painted faces and streamers. She liked the masks and would look at the masks and pretend which character she wanted to be on which day.

The time has passed quickly. She is now in the Midwest and her only child, her daughter Calley has left. Calley has not taken Sundance with her yet but will be back for her. Sundance is the dog of all dogs. Hope loves Sundance fiercely and will miss her. She also misses Calley with a deep longing to one day be near her again.

It is time to take the masks off! It is time to be Hope. No more illusions, no more pretending which character she wants to be.

Hope recalls that she has saved these masks. She pulls out the box with the masks and kisses each mask and then smashes the masks on the hardwood floor one by one. Each mask breaks into pieces. There is something deeply gratifying about this! The pieces lay around the desk where Hope will begin to write her novel.

Hope knows that she wants to write. She wants to write about when Sundance was still living with her and Brad. She wants to write about Calley. She wants to talk about middle age, menopause, empty-nest syndrome, to talk about when death calls you, when love calls you, to discuss fixing your mental health, to talk about rescuing a dog, relocating to another state, and to discuss racial disparity.

There is one more thing... She wants her writing to make an impact. She sits down at her computer. She opens the word document, and she puts her thoughts, her dreams and her everything down onto the pages.

Hope Remembers When Calley Was Here

Sundance stretches and jumps off the bed. She is ready to get up for the day. She greets each family member with a sloppy kiss on the face. She demands attention by looking at you with her big brown, deep eyes which compel you to hold your gaze on her fury face. She has black fur with caramel-colored patches on her face, and specks of white on the end of her paws. Her tail is long and fluffy. Her ears are floppy. She is a rescue dog, but we have never bothered to find out what her breed is. We don't care. We love her just the way she is. We call her Sundance because her eyes dance. Her eyes are dark and sparkle, especially when she is happy. It's a shame that most medium size dogs only live until 15 years of age. We form such a bond and need them longer than that. My daughter describes Sundance as a Mexican and African American dog with a little bit of white based on her coloring.

Calley has been applying for jobs. She loves to travel and would like to get out of the Midwest.

I am happy for my daughter's dreams, but another part of me wishes she would stay. Calley is now in her early twenties. It seems that she was just on the high school basketball team yesterday. The time goes by so fast. I used to be so busy with all of her activities and now that time has passed. Suddenly, I have time where I can go to book festivals, spend more time with friends, go on walks and not have to worry about when I get home. My husband and I have more time together. We are now middle-aged, and the time has gone by so quickly. In the blink of an eye, you realize you are still you, but you have now noticed changes to your body. There are wrinkles under your eyes, dry skin on the back of your arms and more size to your midsection. You move slower, you don't always sleep well, and you realize that your life is already halfway over. It is a scary thought!

"Mom-I got the job and I am heading out west in two days!"

"I am happy for you, and I mean it." This is my outside voice. My inside voice says *no, I cannot lose you. I am not ready to see you go. I relish seeing you each day and cannot imagine my life without your presence.*

I immediately start thinking about how I can move to the state where my only child is. I formulate all of these plans in my head. I will apply for jobs in the same state. I will get an amazing job and will be near my daughter. Unfortunately, my daughter is taking a job where she is not stationed in one state.

Calley's job will require travel to other states as needed. So much for my dreams of relocating to a new state! What if she meets someone and has kids? How will I be near my daughter and grandkids? I cannot keep playing these scenarios in my head. I have to take it one day at time.

Sundance will not be able to go with Calley on her new job yet. Calley is determined that at some point she will get a trailer and a new truck. She will then take Sundance with her.

The day that Cal leaves for her job, my heart feels like it has been sucked out of my body. I feel weak and dizzy. I sit down at my desk. I kick the broken masks on the floor with my shoe until they break into a thousand more pieces. The pieces represent the pieces of my new life which I no longer know. A puddle of my tears fall onto the floor and splatter like rain drops.

This is my child for whom I have spent years watching her every move! This is a move I do not get to be a part of. I watch her van pull out of the driveway. It feels surreal. It hurts like an unrecognizable pain. I cannot identify this pain as there is no familiarity to it. It is the pain of loss. The pain of everything that is familiar slipping away from you. Everything on the inside of me wants my child back near me where I can see her more often.

Sundance barks and I get up from my office chair and close the door to my office. I reach for Sundance, but she pulls back from me. She wants Calley and she stares me down with a hard look questioning who took my daughter away from her. I stroke her thick fur and I kiss her. She lays in my arms like putty.

Brad and I carry Sundance to the car and take her to her favorite dog park. This park does not help her today. She goes to the fence at the park, lays down, and focuses her gaze on the basketball hoop near the park. She is searching for Calley who used to shoot hoops there.

I think about all the times I have gone to the dog park with Calley, and I find myself staring at the basketball hoop with Sundance in search of my daughter who is no longer here. Brad misses her too, but it is different when you are a stepparent. The connection to the child is not always the same as if it were your biological child.

Is the House You Enter Happy or Sad?

I am still thinking about Calley when I hear my phone. *Ring, ring.* I pick up the phone and listen to my mother-in-law who lost her husband seven years ago. She is still devastated by the loss. She misses having someone in the house with her. She is now all alone. It is hard for her to sleep at night. She remembers when her husband would tuck her in at night and tell her he loved her. She would do anything to hear these words again. She has saved a recording of his voice which she plays every day. The loss of a loved one is overwhelming. My mother-in-law does not like to go home at night because the house is empty. She works all day at a very busy school. She then goes shopping or meets friends or family. She has trouble sitting or relaxing because if she stops, then she has to think. When she thinks, she thinks of him and their previous life. If she keeps moving, it blocks the thoughts from entering her mind. I worry that she is not sleeping enough, not eating enough. I am concerned she is out late in the dark nights walking because she cannot sleep. I talk to her about all of these things. We have decided that she will sleep at our house on a weekend night. I see that she sleeps when she is here. Her job invigorates her, and she loves the people and children whom she works with. It is the after part that worries me. What happens when she goes home? There is no one there anymore. Yet, she will not leave the house as the memories live there. She has so many memories of when her son was growing up, so many thoughts of when her husband was alive. There is now a quiet in her home that she never wished for and has never known. She starts thinking of houses with more depth now. When she goes into a house, she wants to know if it feels happy or sad? I want to help her but know she must want to help herself. There is no easy fix. Mental Health counseling and medicine, whether it is a combination of western or homeopathic would probably help to balance her hormones. I have asked her to please go to seek help. I have told her I will go with her. She does not want to go, and I cannot force her. I wish for a miracle each day.

Hot Flashes That Beat Me Down!

I am soaked with sweat as I take a walk with friends. I cannot sleep at night. I lay in the bed for hours. The hot flashes come and go as I lay in my bed. My mood swings are like a loose broken swing that rocks back and forth. I have become unhinged! I think I can fix this. It will go away on its own. I will work through this...

Months later I crawl into my doctor's office and beg for quality of life. I am beat down. My eyes have circles under them from lack of sleep. I no longer know who or what I am. My anxiety is on a level higher than I have ever known. Tears well up in my broken eyes as I try to combat the mood swings without medication.

My doctor helps me to create a homeopathic remedy, combined with western medicine to treat the mood swings, anxiety, and insomnia. He suggests therapy.

I have never done therapy. I want to say no to therapy, but it makes sense. I welcome anything that will take me back to a snippet of my previous life that I knew prior to my current condition.

The combination of treatment takes time to work. The hot flashes still occur but are milder, my sleep has improved, my anxiety has decreased. I had many restless nights when this first came on. I would hardly sleep due to the insomnia. I thought I was going to lose my mind. I am so thankful I sought medical help.

No one talks about menopause. For some women, they do not have difficulty and for others, it is awful. I now know why a woman might go outside and lay naked in a snowbank to cool her body off while going through the hot flashes. I have a very real sense of what it means to feel weird during this time. I have now also started therapy for the first time in my life to help with my mental health. I think these are good things and very important to do so that you can get yourself in a good mental state.

I have gone with a shorter hairstyle as I go through menopause, my hair is becoming thinner which is another reason to keep my hair shorter. I have dark brown hair with streaks of red that my hairdresser puts in as highlights. The back is a short bob where the front is longer on the sides. I have bangs. Calley and I do not go to the same hairdresser as she prefers someone of color. She feels like they can work with her hair better.

When my parents named me, they named me Hope. Hope is an English feminine name derived from the Old English word hopian referring to a positive expectation or to the theological virtue of hope. I try to live by what my name means. There are days that I find it hard to live up to my name's sake. On these days, I reflect on what my name means and strive to do better.

Empty-Nest Syndrome

I picture Calley putting on her sneakers and her name brand athletic wear. She is headed to the dog park with Sundance. Calley has always had great taste in clothes and shoes. She is very careful about the brands she buys. She wants high quality, but it does not have to come at a high price. Most of her shopping is done online. Her favorite item to shop for is shoes. She has an amazing shoe collection, which she has worked hard on over the years. Her shoes are all in their original boxes with the receipts inside. Calley has an athletic build. She likes to work out. She has now started eating differently. She recently became vegan. Her stepdad and I have been vegan for a decade, but I never thought she would become vegan as well. It was a movie about athletes eating a vegan lifestyle that hooked her. She saw how much more energy they had after eating this way. I was shocked. I wanted her to become vegan for years. She has diabetes on both sides of her family. I am hoping the way she eats now will help her to avoid diabetes.

Cal likes my vegan chili and asparagus. I am cooking the chili now. Part of the chili recipe involves blending walnuts. I cut up the jalapeno, add the tomatoes, spices and then slow cook it on the stove top for about an hour. I cook my asparagus in the oven. I have found a Cajun spice that I like to put on the asparagus prior to cooking it. I am remembering cooking this meal before Calley left for her new job. Now she is away at her job. I am still cooking, but now it is just for myself and my husband. I haven't figured out the portion sizes yet. When it was the three of us, I never had leftovers. Now, I always have leftovers. I have to learn how to decrease the amount of food I am making.

I am in the empty-nest phase of my life. The empty-nest stage is where you find you again. It's a hard place but can also be a good place to get to. It's a matter of how you approach it. Nobody talks about it. When Cal first left, I cried. I felt like a shell of myself. A voice inside of me said this is it, we have one life to live. Choose how to best live it, make a difference in the world. I wanted her to stay in this town; selfish on my part because I love to see her. Her dad also loves to see her. Calley is a child of two worlds. I think she is trying to figure out how to make both worlds collide. It is not easy. Should I have thought more about her two worlds when I was raising her? I was young and did not think of the consequences. It is when you get older that your mind thinks about the life you have lived and what's left, what you could have done differently.

I am realizing as I age how quickly life goes by. I am now seeing more closely how death affects a person. I am surrounded by people who have lost a loved one or are worried about what their life will look like when their loved one goes. I am thinking more deeply about what I want to do with my life as I age. I have always loved to write. Being an author would be the ultimate dream for me. For example, I told my therapist that I love to write, and I have begun to write again. She commended me. "What stopped you from writing before?" she asked.

"I was so busy with my job, my daughter, and my husband. "What is stopping you now?" she continued.

"Nothing I say. I find writing invigorating. It gives me life. Writing is everything. It is not difficult; it is as effortless as a leaf falling off of a tree. Writing is magical and it takes me to another place. The creative part in my mind where I can make the characters jump off the pages."

Sundance is a rescue dog. We have decided we want more. We move out into the country in our Midwestern town. We buy an old farmhouse. Guess who rescues the dogs? It is Cal. Sundance was rescued in Florida during a hurricane. I am not sure if there could ever be a better dog than Sundance. She is so loyal, so protective. She loves deep. I guess I am about to find out about other dogs. Calley is going to bring us a dog she calls Sugar. This dog was rescued in Arizona where Calley is currently working. Sugar is a mix, perhaps part Pitbull. We really do not know, nor do we care. She is brown, medium size, green eyes, and has a short tail. Calley trained Sundance and she has also been training Sugar. I think she relates better to animals than people. She does an incredible job of dog training. She has so many skills, but a professional dog trainer could also be one of them. I like being in the old farmhouse. The yard can hold so many more dogs. We also have a beautiful view of the sky at night. I have more room to garden. I know I do not want to be in the Midwest forever. I am grateful for my time here now. I have family and friends here. One day want to be near a mountain. I want to write while looking out at a mountain. It is a reoccurring dream that I have. I can picture the yellow kitchen, the sheer white curtains in the kitchen window and the breeze blowing in as I sit at the wooden table and write my next book. Calley is somewhere close by. She loves the mountains. I will get to see her more often, but that means I will get to see the family and friends I am near now less often. I do not know when this will happen. For now, I will just make the most of my time here.

Thoughts of Calley

I picture Calley's face in my head. She is so beautiful, as are all biracial children. She has thick dark hair, long eye lashes. Her skin is magical. It is the color of skin that I used to lay out in the sun for hours to obtain her natural hue. Calley keeps her hair medium length. She has red highlights at the ends of her dark hair. Calley no longer straightens her hair. It is too much work. She lets the natural waves tumble loosely. It makes her feel white when she straightens her hair. She prefers to feel more like her father's family. Her dad is dark. He is from Guyana. It's funny because she grew up in the Midwest and has always seen her dad who lived in Florida, but for most of her life, did not live with him. Even though, my immediate family is here in the Midwest, Calley has always related to people of color. Perhaps, it was the fact that he wasn't directly in her life for many years. He was her biggest hero. She loved his cars, his love of dogs. He ran his own business where he worked on cars. Calley always admired this as well. She wanted to be her own boss. She struggled to work under others. She wanted to have the control. I wonder should I have stayed with Calley's dad? Did I not give her enough of what she needed when she was growing up? Southern Florida has more diversity. Was I wrong to bring her to the Midwest? I never thought about these questions when she was born. She was everything I always wanted. Race was not ever a factor for me. I always wanted a biracial child. I did not think of what life is like for them. I always thought of them as the most fortunate kids in the world. They looked different, had beautiful skin and hair. I even wished I was biracial at one time or another in my life.

Tonight, I am making vegan enchiladas with rice and beans. I enjoy this dish. I think of Calley as I make it. She also enjoys this dish. The beans are great for a vegan. They are a good source of protein. I picture Calley at the table with her Yellowstone National Park shirt on, her shorts that match, and her Nike slides. I also envision her dark eyes, with long eyelashes, her beautiful dark, thick eyebrows, her wavy hair, her full lips, and wide nose. Calley has long legs and is 5"7. Her build is very muscular and athletic. She has one dimple on her right side when she smiles. Cal has perfect teeth and a smile that lights the room. She has been buying and wearing national park shirts and caps. She loves the national parks. She has traveled to so many of them. She is a self-taught hiker. She also maps out her entire trips to various states by herself. This includes where she will wash up, get food, hike and where she can park her van to sleep. Calley is a kick-ass type of girl. She wants to call her own shots and make her own mark on the world.

Cal really embraced the national parks as she got older. She loved the adrenaline rush of hiking up and down mountains. She enjoyed the peace that comes from within a beautiful area such as a national park. She took pictures of the animals and the scenery. Her pictures took my breath away. They are so precise and perfect. Calley is a perfectionist; and this comes through in her pictures. Calley has taken Sundance on many hikes in the mountains. Sundance likes to hike and can keep up with Cal. She has also gotten into mountain biking. I recall her last trip to Idaho where she was mountain biking on a trail by herself. A stranger found her phone on the trail with no sign of Calley. The stranger found my number and called me. At first when the stranger called, I thought it was Calley, wanting it to be her. Even said, I know this is you, stop playing tricks on me! The good ending to this tale was that Calley had made her way to town and was able to send me an e-mail from there. She told me she was ok. The stranger told me he would drop her phone off at the local police station. How fortunate that she was safe and even got her phone back! In the back of my mind, I say what if this was not the ending of this tale? What if something had happened to my daughter while she was mountain biking on a dangerous trail by herself? What would I do? I have come to the realization that people have passions they need to fulfill, and you cannot stop them. You must let them live out their dreams. I do hope one day she has someone on the trail with her, someone who can save her if she is hurt.

A Simple Life?

As the days go by, I talk to Calley daily and she likes her job. She is making good money and she is proud. I understand that I have to let her live her best life, whatever that looks like to her.

Calley is happy with her job as a National Park Ranger. She feels like she is doing something she is passionate about. She is a Protection Ranger who is tasked with keeping the park and visitors safe through law enforcement, emergency medical services, firefighting and search and rescue. Park Rangers who work for the National Park Service may be required to work in remote areas and travel across the country to work in different parks. Cal could never see herself in a daily 9-5 job. It was too mundane for her. She needed the excitement and sheer thrill of adventure that this job will bring her. The job is dangerous, and I worry. I know this job is a good fit for her and therefore, as a mom, I must accept it. We have to let our kids grow, to explore, to live life. We will not be in their lives forever and they must create their own. I wish Calley's life would be simple, such as living in a home near me, working a local job, and when she is ready, getting married and having kids. I dream of what her baby boy would look like, a full head of wavy dark hair, big brown eyes, and a brown complexion. I fantasize about her husband. Would he also be biracial, perhaps Hispanic, or some other race? Could he be white? I do not think so. Cal will most likely marry a person of color, like herself. Why, because she identifies best with people of color.

Calley told me the story about one time when she was on a bus in our town. She was with her white friend, Jenny. An older African American man approached them on the bus.

"Why are you two together? You are different from one another. You cannot hang out."

The man's comments hit Calley like a brick. Soon after that she started hanging out with more friends of color. Calley talks to me about when she visits Guyana, how she loves it because there are not so many white people everywhere. She tells me how when she drives in our downtown Iowa where there is a major university, how privileged these kids are. They do not even realize it. She continues to explain that in Guyana people are fortunate if they have a washer and dryer, clean drinking water and indoor plumbing. Calley has become so knowledgeable of other cultures outside of small-town USA. I think about many of her comments. I realize I want to talk about them. If you do not discuss things like this; it will not cause people to think. Sometimes I remind Calley, you have some white in you too, from my side. I then realize this is petty. Her comments are from the heart, and I need to listen, and try to make the world better for her. She is entitled to the way she sees herself. My job as a mother is to realize that the stories, she has told me are because of the various things in her life experiences. I see her as the most striking child in the world. There are others that due to the color of her skin, perceive her differently.

Dru

Brad and I are going to pick up my mother-in-law tonight to take her out to eat. Tomorrow will be the seventh anniversary of my father-in-law's death. She is trying to keep very busy. The busyness does not kill the pain in her eyes, face, jaw, and neck. We try to put a small dent in her pain. I am not sure we are succeeding. It's almost like putting a bandage on a broken heart. So many days I ask myself, what can I do to help her? The answer is always the same. She has to help herself. What if she is a person that is a giver and has never taken time for herself, only for others? How do we get her to help herself? I think she should see a professional therapist, but thus far she has continued to refuse.

After our meal, Dru comes back to our house and will sleep over tonight. I go to get her some tea, but when I look on the couch, she is already passed out. Her colored brown hair is medium length with a little gray on the sides. She is very slim as she does a lot of walking. She does not drive. Her husband did the driving, but she now rides the bus. I notice her phone is ringing. I do something I would normally never do; I answer her phone. A stranger with a deep voice asks for Dru. I explain that she is sleeping. I ask for his name. His name is Cornelius. Funny, I have never heard her mention his name before. I will have to ask her another day about who this mystery man is.

It turns out my opportunity to ask about Cornelius comes sooner than I had anticipated. I am driving her home and I say, "By the way, your phone rang last night, and I picked it up. Cornelius asked that I tell you that he called."

Dru looks away, embarrassed as if I am entering an area of her life that was never to be disclosed. "Hope, he is my good friend" she says.

I can tell from the way that she says, "good friend," that he is more than that. I nod quietly. How did you meet? "

"I met him at a peace rally."

My mother-in-law has always been an activist.

"We have coffee together from time to time."

"I would love to meet him one day. What does he look like?"

"He is tall, African American, gray braids, wears combat boots and jeans."

My father-in-law was white. My mother-in-law is also white, but she has always loved African Americans. She wants to change the world and make it a better place for them. What an interesting match! Dru tells me that she will never love again. My father-in-law was the love of her life. She does not believe that you can love more than once. I hope that Cornelius can change her mind. She has been so sad since my father-in-law passed. What if she could give love another chance? We only live once. Shouldn't we try to make the best of our lives? Horrible things happen. Do we persevere or give up? We know death is a part of life. Do we accept it, or do we say life did us wrong? I think this depends on who we are as an individual. It also depends on our mental health. If our mental health is declining, it is good to see an expert.

Calley Brings Sugar Home!

Sugar is here. Calley is here! Cal cannot stay long due to the requirements of her job. We will have one week with her. Sugar is three years old. Sundance is 4 years old. They are both girls. Sugar is nervous, except around Cal. Sundance is so excited to see Calley. She gives her a hug and follows her around. Sundance is jealous of Sugar for the first three days. We let Sugar and Sundance interact. It does not go so well at first. Slowly, there is a small change. They start to hang around each other in the yard. Sugar is starting to get used to us. She will come to us when we call her name. I'm not sure I can love any dog as much as I have loved Sundance but must admit I would like to have another one. I think the closeness in age was a good move.

Calley seems to like the old farmhouse. She likes being able to run around with the dogs and the freedom of more space. Her dark wavy hair is in a ponytail, and she has one of her national parks caps on with one of her national park shirts. She has on a pair of Nike jogging pants and is wearing her latest Nike athletic shoes.

Sundance and Sugar are two different dogs. Sundance will chase the ball and bring it back. She loves people, and children. She likes human attention. Sugar prefers the attention of other dogs. She is constantly in Sundance's space. Sugar will not fetch a ball. She does like to chase Sundance around the yard. The one exception for both dogs is Calley. They both love Cal. I am beginning to think Cal might be part dog. She has such a way with dogs. The dogs growl at one another as Calley enters the yard. Both dogs want her ultimate attention. Sundance and Sugar love when Calley is around. It means freedom, playing ball, and playing with them. Calley likes to run in the yard and both dogs try to catch her. Sundance can catch her. Sugar cannot accomplish this yet.

Calley and I take a ride in Calley's truck with Sundance and Sugar. Both dogs like to ride in Calley's truck. Sundance puts her head out the open window in the passenger seat. Sugar is in the backseat on the driver's side. Sugar keeps her head in the truck. Sundance sneaks over to the driver's side and lays her head on Calley's lap as Calley drives. I am in the back with Sugar, and I watch her peek in on Calley and Sundance from the passenger seat. Both dogs have smiles on their faces.

After the ride in the truck, we decide to give Sundance a break from Sugar. Brad, Calley and I go to the dog park with Sundance. Calley has trained Sundance since she was a puppy how to interact at dog parks. Cal said Sugar is not ready for the dog parks yet. She is too aggressive. Sundance keeps to herself at the dog parks but will occasionally interact with the other dogs. She will run with them or chase a ball with the other dogs. She has always loved the dog parks, which is why we still go to the parks with her. Time at the dog parks is so enjoyable and peaceful with Sundance.

When we arrive back at the farmhouse, Calley, Sundance and Sugar head to bed. I glance in Calley's room and observe that Sundance sleeps so that she can watch Calley as she sleeps. She wants to protect her. Sugar sleeps at the foot of the bed with her eyes on Sundance and Calley.

Calley Meets Cornelius

I have not seen Calley this content in years. She is doing her thing, running the show the way, she wants. She enjoys her job. She loves the travel the job gives her. Her brown skin is glowing. Her eyes sparkle. Her body is in great shape. Her job is very physical, and she also works out. She is eating very healthy as she finds this provides her with more energy. She incorporates nuts, fruit, beans, and plant-based protein into her way of eating. It is so good to have her home. When she is not looking, I gaze at her so that I can form a permanent picture of Calley in my head. I wonder if she will date someone soon. How will they meet? What will he look like? When will I meet him? Will he be a dog lover and a vegan?

Brad and I go with Calley to visit my Mother-in-law. Cal wants to see her while she is in town. As we pull up to Grandma Dru's house, we see Cornelius is there. I know he is there because I see his lime green mountain bike in the front yard. Cornelius steps outside and I introduce him to Calley. He and Calley began to talk about Ital food. Ital food is a natural way of cooking that tries to avoid processed food, additives, oil, salt, and sugar, and was developed by Rastafarians.

Cornelius eats Ital food at the local Jamaican restaurant. Calley has had it several times in Florida and loves it. Dru steps outside and runs to Cal and embraces her. She has missed Calley so much! We sit in Dru's front yard around her table and talk. There is reggae music playing in the background. Cornelius likes reggae music. He is teaching Dru how to dance to it. I want to learn too. Dance is a way to free the body and the mind. It is a beautiful gift. Dru dances with Cornelius. She has a light smile on her face. Calley watches, intrigued as she has never seen Brad's mother this free spirited. Neither have I. I think this is the power of dance. It is when you stop dancing that the magical feeling goes away which is why you must keep dancing.

We head back to our farmhouse. I am feeling hopeful about Dru and Cornelius. There is no romance going on, only a friendship. I see the flicker of hope in each of their eyes for something more.

I have come to find out that Cornelius was married. He married someone he loved for fifty-one years and unfortunately, she passed away from cancer about two years ago. He is in his seventies and believes that he would rather live out the rest of his life with a partner rather than being alone. He needs someone to be there to talk with in the mornings and in the evenings. He has political events that he wants a soulmate to attend with him. He wants a dancing partner. His wife was his reggae teacher. She was from Jamaica. He loved her deeply and misses her. He never thought he would seek the attention of a white woman. It just happened, so unexpectedly. The biggest dilemma for him is he is now ready to form more than a friendship with Dru. Dru is not ready. She is waiting for her dead husband to come back to life in her dreams. She wants to talk with him and know that he is ok and not hurting. What if there is a heaven and he is waiting there for her? Should she constantly feel guilty that he died, but she lived?

Cal drives us back home from Dru's house. She is playing hip hop music as she drives. Calley has an extensive playlist. She likes rap, hip hop, reggae, soul train, and some southern rock. She will also listen to Latin music, but she does not speak Spanish. The language of Guyana is English and therefore, her father does not speak Spanish.

A Week Gone Too Quick!

The next morning, I am in the kitchen making vegan waffles. with toppings to include strawberries, walnuts, blueberries, and bananas.

Calley is going to help me with the garden today. We have much more space now. We will plant tomato plants, jalapenos, red and green peppers, carrots, green onions, and zucchini. I am looking forward to planting. It is relaxing and rewarding. This year, I want to take any extra produce to families in need.

Sugar and Sundance watch us as we till the soil for the garden. They both seem content. After the gardening is done, we go on a hike. The hikes are not what Calley is used to. She is used to the mountains. We looked at many of her pictures last night. The pictures of the mountains are so beautiful and clean. Calley explains that it is about getting into a wilder environment where you can enjoy nature and push yourself physically.

Brad and I are sitting outside, tired from the hike. I thought Calley would be tired, but we are now watching Cal work on detailing a car that we have had for years. The car looks like new when she finishes with it. She also has products that she uses on the car that has kept it from rusting. I admire her work. She still goes to car shows when she has time. She can also do some mechanical work on cars such as oil changes and brake jobs.

She talks about her job as a park ranger. She loves the travel, deeply cares about the parks and preserving them. She met someone that she works with who has asked her out multiple times. He is tall, about 6'2, muscular, dark skinned, has long, thick dark hair. His name is Dakota, and he is Native American. He is two years older than Calley. He asked her to go hiking with him in the mountains.

"What did you say?"

"I said no"

"Why?"

"I do not want to date someone that I work with."

"I understand that, but he sounds perfect for you. Is there a rule that you cannot date because you work together?"

"No, there is not. I just don't feel like putting in the effort."

"Calley, everyone needs someone at some point in their lives. It's good to try and see if Dakota might be a good match for you."

Interesting, I think to myself. I never pictured her with a Native American, but as I think about it, it makes sense. Dakota sounds like someone who loves the land and cherishes it. This alone would mean the world to Calley. He sounds very handsome and stubborn. They could really butt heads, or they could be perfect for one another.

We stop at our local Jamaican restaurant to get Ital food. Today, we get Jamaican curried tofu with chickpeas. It is filling and nurturing. Unfortunately, there are not many Jamaican restaurants in the Midwest.

I see Cornelius coming in as we are leaving so I stop to talk with him. He shares with me that he was hoping Dru would meet him today, but she canceled.

"Why did she cancel?"

"She said she felt like we were together too often, and she was not ready for this."

He asks Brad if he will talk to his mom. Brad explains it is probably easier for me to talk to Dru. It's more of a woman-to-woman thing. We say goodbye to Cornelius. Cal tells me she likes him, and it would be good for Grandma Dru to date him. I explain to Calley that Grandma Dru still misses Denny and feels she could never date anyone else. She feels there is only one true love for each of us. Calley says that is definitely not true in the animal kingdom. Thoughts to ponder…

Calley is driving back to the farmhouse and blasting the song "*Ain't No Mountain High Enough.*" This is one of our favorite songs.

"Mom, music is a gift."

"Yes, I feel it is one of the most precious gifts that life gives us."

"I can get lost in the music".

"Me too Calley, me too."

We talk about new artists coming out with new albums. We like similar artists. I actually like Calley's music playlist better than my own.

As Calley pulls up in the driveway, we notice a package.

"Did you order something Cal?"

"No, I did not order anything."

"This package is addressed to you."

She opens it. Inside, is a pair of beautiful hiking shoes. There is a card on top, which says to the girl I want to hike with, no more excuses. I smile and say Dakota must have sent you these.

"She smiles. "Looks like he did, guess I will have to go hiking with him and once I beat him up and down the mountain, he will go away."

"Or maybe he will stay for round two," I say.

She shrugs her shoulders and heads inside with her new boots. I noticed that he picked her boot color and style. She is not easy to pick for and I am impressed. Now, I wonder, will I meet him? I guess I will have to tuck that thought aside and see how things transpire.

Calley, Sundance and Sugar go to sleep early again. I look into Calley's room while she is sleeping. Both dogs are watching over her. Her eyes are closed, and she is sound asleep. I remember when she was little, and I would gaze at her. Again, the most beautiful child is always what comes to my mind. I am so content to have her home for this short time. I am trying to make the most out of each day while she is here. I am anxious to hang out with her all day. I know that there are friends and family that want to see her too. She has a big family here on my side, including many cousins. She is the only biracial one. I never thought about it, but she told me she wished she had other biracial cousins. She loves them deeply but feels that she is different from them. As I lay down in my bed, I try to imagine how that must feel, but I can't comprehend this.

The morning sunrise shines throughout the farmhouse. The sunlight is powerful. It produces a glow on everything it touches. I am in our yellow kitchen with the large windows, looking outside. I love the morning sunshine. It means the day has just started. The sunshine produces positive vibes and energy. We have lots of windows which increases the amount of sun that pours into our house. I do yoga and workouts in the mornings. We have a room set up in our basement with workout equipment. I have been doing this for years and believe in exercising. Calley joins me today for yoga. I normally do a slower paced yoga whereas Calley always does the intense yoga. I do the intense yoga with her today. It is difficult but I do feel refreshed upon completion.

She is going into town today to visit her cousins and is looking forward to seeing them. They are going to play basketball and do some shopping. She will spend the entire day with them. The time has gone by so rapidly and her week is almost up.

I am sad that she is leaving tomorrow, but so grateful for the time I have spent with her. I guess this is our new normal. I want to plan when I will see her next, but I know due to her job, she does not know when that will be.

Calley Leaves for Arizona

It is early in the morning and Calley is awake and packing up her belongings. Sundance and Sugar are moping around the house. They sense that Cal is heading out. They follow her around the house. She reminds me how she is saving for a truck and a camper, so Sundance can travel with her. Sundance and Calley have a bond that is unbreakable. Calley works with other park rangers who have campers and their dogs travel with them. She hates leaving Sundance but knows she will have the money to buy the truck and camper in about 8 months. In the meantime, she will come home as she can to see Sugar and Sundance. I don't know how I will cope when Sundance leaves. She is an amazing dog. She is patient, beautiful and fun. Sugar will stay with Brad and I. Sugar is also a great dog. She is impatient, adorable and beats to her own drum.

Calley has a long drive to Arizona, which will be about twenty-two hours from our midwestern town. She loves to drive. She is a good driver. She demands control of the road and listens to her music. She will sometimes listen to various podcasts.

We embrace Calley and wish her safe travels. Tears are in my eyes as she is again on the road and off on her own. After she leaves, I go and workout in our basement. This helps me in so many ways; it helps to wake me up and boost my endurance.

Calley's phone rings and she answers, "What's up dad? I am driving back to Arizona. I miss you too. Maybe, I will try to come to Florida soon, but I would rather meet you in Guyana. Talk to you soon and love you."

Calley thinks to herself about Guyana. She likes the Capuchin monkeys, Caribbean red beans and rice, the coconut water, and of course the mountains. There are areas to hike and there are not a lot of people everywhere. There are also more brown and black people. She really enjoyed the recent trip she took with her dad there. It is a simple way of life, and she may build something on the land that her dad owns. She may choose to live in Guyana.

Calley thinks to herself, *eventually, I would like to live in Guyana. I am young now and need to make money, but this may be where I will be in the future. I know my mom loves me and she is going to come see me wherever I am.* Cal is playing reggae music, and this too reminds her of Guyana.

Calley also thinks about her mom and stepdad's home. *It was good to be home. It felt so good to see Sundance. Damn, I love that dog. Sugar is good too, but she plays too much. She needs to listen more. Sundance will do anything that I ask her to do. I have hiked mountains with her off leash and she kept up and stayed by my side. I miss all my friends and family at home, but I don't want to live there anymore. I love to travel. I hope to travel through all of the United States and then do some international travel too, outside of Guyana.*

The job I have now is good. I feel like we are a tight group. I feel respected and love being outdoors. I do like Dakota. He is fine as hell. Not only that, but he also picked out hiking boots that were perfect. I know I have high standards when it comes to shoes, but I have never seen anyone pick a pair of shoes that I love. Why does Dakota have to be in the group of park rangers that I work with? It's hard. I try to play my feelings down for him, but I am struggling. I have never felt this way about a man before. He is different from most guys. He loves the outdoors and I know we have a lot in common. I know he likes me; I am going to have to think of more ways to avoid him. I don't need a man. If I meet someone later and I am older and ready for it, that's a different story. Right now, I just don't have time.

I just don't want to get involved with anyone. I feel like if I date, this person will destroy my dreams. Maybe I am selfish, but I got to do the things I want to do and do them my way. I mean, damn, you only live once!

I think of my friends who are in their twenties, and they have kids. Their lives are over. They don't have freedom like I do now. I don't want to report to someone. I am not good with this. I don't need to have authority. I need people to listen to me. The only reason I am ok with reporting to my boss now is because he is different from my other bosses. He is dark skinned, and he reminds me of myself when he gives orders. I am good with him. My boss also has respect for me. He knows I know how to do my job and that I am mechanical and smart as shit. He knows that when he hired me, he got the best.

Many More Thoughts in Calley's Head

So many more thoughts race through Calley's mind as she continues her drive to
Arizona

*I have some time before I have to get back to work. I planned it this way so that I could do
some hiking. There are two trails that I want to hit. I have built this into my schedule. These will
be new trails to me so that is exciting! I can even wear my new kicks. Now that I am vegan, I am
fast on the trails. I cannot believe how much better my body feels. I never thought I would say this
or go vegan, but I am for real. I even got my dad to eat vegan while we were in Guyana. I know he
did it to please me, but I hope it helped him out too. I wish he would keep doing it, but I doubt it. I
am glad my mom and stepdad introduced me to this way of eating. I will probably never tell them
this, but it was one of the best things I have ever done. I would like to get other people of color to
eat this way. I talk about it to my friends, but not one of them have done it. I heard Dakota tell
someone he was trying to go vegan. He is close to my age. That is unbelievable and makes me like
him even more. What are the odds of this? It's almost like we were destined to meet.*

*I took some great pics of Sundance. When I get to missing her, I look at these pics. I took
some pics of Sugar too. I think it is good for Sundance to have Sugar. Eventually, I will take Sun-
dance on the road. That's my dog and I need her. Maybe I will rescue more dogs. My mom and
stepdad now have the room to hold rescue dogs on that old farmhouse property.*

*I have also built some time into my return trip so that I can stop at the outlet stores and
look at the shoes. I always make sure I get there early in the morning so that I am the first in line.
I love shoes. I like adding to my shoe collection. I have even purchased some shoes and been able
to sell them for more. I have only done this twice because I love shoes so much that it's hard for
me to part with them.*

*There's my jam. One of my favorite songs just came on. This really relaxes me when driving.
There is a Mexican restaurant. I am going to stop and get some vegan tacos, rice, and beans. I go*

into this little hole in the wall restaurant. The owners are Mexican so I know the food will be good. I am not disappointed.

I stop at the outlet mall next. I find some nice kicks. I can't sell these. These will be mine for my shoe collection. I take a pic and send it to my mom. She also is a shoe lover, so she gets it.

In an hour, I arrive at the hiking trail. There are not many hikers on it. I like it like this. It is quiet and peaceful. I have already mapped out this trail and the figured out how long it will take me to hike it. I like doing this. I am in charge. I put on my new hiking boots, tie my hair back in a ponytail. I put on one of my caps and I am ready! I carry a backpack with water and snacks. It is a lightweight backpack. I have my camera because I love to take pictures of wildlife. I do carry a pocketknife and bear spray. The scenery is beautiful. It is really like I am removed from the world when I hike. I hike for three hours. I head back to my van. I have mapped out a spot where I can sleep. Good thing I built up the back of my van. I have a cot and bins for my clothes. I have a sleeping bag and pillows. I have really worked hard on making my van very comfortable so that I can sleep in it.

I wake up early and see a family of deer near where I am parked. There is another trail that I want to hike. It will take be forty-five minutes to drive there. I put on some rap music and head to the next trail. I am anxious to see this trail because it is also new to me. When I arrive at the trail, there are a lot of people there. I map out a path that will take me away from all of the people. I prefer to hike on my own. I like to go at a fast speed and like to do it my way. I used to call my mom from the top of mountains, but she asked me to stop doing this. I have climbed a lot of moun-tains. It always feels like a victory.

These hiking shoes are incredible! I have more cushioning that I have had with some of my other hiking shoes. The shoes make my hikes even better!

Now it's time for me to drive. I have to head back to my job. I am looking forward to going back to work. I like to keep busy. This job has really been a good fit for me. I don't remember that last time I said I was looking forward to getting back to work. I'm glad I took this job. It was hard to leave everyone, but the travel is dope. I do not know when I will get to travel like this again. I might as well do it while I am young. I am seeing so many people, places, different foods, different cultures. It really opens my eyes to in a way that I have never experienced before. I definitely feel more worldly and well-traveled. I have also learned so much from the hikers that I come across on the various trails and from the park rangers that I work with. I feel like a new me. It's funny how much you can change from your teenage years to your early twenties. I never thought I would see myself living like this, but I got to admit, I like it.

My grandma Dru is very dependent on people. She is my favorite grandma, but I wish she would not depend so much on others. I feel like you have to be independent. Maybe, I have be-come too independent. It was good to see my grandma. I call her almost every day. She is a *talker, so I try to listen and take some time for her. I know she is lonely now that my grandpa is no longer here.*

I like Cornelius. I also like that fact that he is black. I think grandma should date him. She is stubborn though and I do not know if she will date him. She would probably feel guilty to date someone else. I would like to think that if one day my husband died, I could love again. My grandma tells me I could not. My mom tells me I could. My mom says that it is important to go on and if that means dating again, then that is ok. She says love come into our lives in many different ways and at many different times.

I know I am young still, but I find myself thinking about a lot of things. Maybe it has to do with hiking. When I hike, it as though I have been transported to another world. It is so freeing. No one around to give you orders, you plan your route, and you plan how you long your hike will be. I do notice that sometimes I am the only person of color on the trails. This really depends on where I am hiking. It used to bother me, but now I have grown used to it. Maybe if I ever have kids, I will teach them about the mountains. I would have to start them at a young age. I did not start hiking in the mountains until I was in my twenties. I wish I had started sooner.

Why Did I Have to Run into That Fine Ass Man!

I have made good time driving and I am almost back to the national park where I am working. I see an area that I have never noticed before. It is beautiful and I have time to stop and check it out. I get out of my van and notice a nice ass Tacoma truck which is what I am saving for. The color is blue. I want to get a black one. I look at the landscape. It is so peaceful. Hardly anyone around. I walk around. There is someone in the water. I like to do that when I am hiking. It cools me off. I take a closer look. It is Dakota. I want to run off and play like I did not see him, but I can't. He has already seen me.

"Hi Calley, how did you like the boots I sent you?"

"Hi Dakota, I loved them. Thank you."

"I thought you would, and I see you got them on."

"Yes, I have been doing some hiking on my way back and then I saw this area which I had not noticed before and had to check it out."

"It's a beautiful area. It's my first time here too. Want to hike together?"

Every bone in my body wants to make up some excuse, but I have run out of them.

I also never have been one-on-one with Dakota.

It's awkward and at the same time, amazing.

"Yes, we can hike together. You know I am a fast hiker, and I might leave you behind on the trail."

"Calley, why do you always have to compete? Why don't you slow down so someone can talk to you? "

"I could do that. I have been driving for hours. Probably be good for me to slow down."

"I never thought I would hear you say that. Good, let's hike."

"Let's do the roughest trail."

"Of course, Calley, I would expect no less from you. You are one of them kick-ass girls."

I smile and say to myself, I know I am.

"How was your trip home?"

"I have two homes, one in the Midwest with my mom and stepdad and one in Florida with my dad. I also consider Guyana my home cause that is where my dad is from, and I have been there several times. Guess, I have three homes. This trip to see my mom and my stepdad was good. My dog, Sundance was there, and I love my dog."

"You know, I have been to Guyana, and I love it."

My heart is racing. I did not know this, and I am shocked to hear this. "What were you doing in Guyana?"

"I was adopted by two white parents when I was three years old. They are the only parents I have ever known, and I love them. My dad loves to do international travel and Guyana is one of his favorite places to go, so that is how I learned about it. "

"Dang, that is interesting. I would have never guessed you were adopted. What happened to your parents?"

"I do not know. I decided not to dig up my past. My adopted parents always showed me love and I was good with that."

"Did it bother you that they were white?"

"Sometimes, I wished they looked just like me and I felt strange, but when I saw how deeply they loved me, it faded."

"I guess I can relate to that because my mom is white, and my dad is Guyanese. I used to wish my mom was from Guyana too, but I also saw that she loved me. She also told me that she wished she looked more like me. She has always told me that my skin and my hair were beautiful. "

"It sounds like your mom is deep."

"She is and I love her and appreciate her. I just don't always tell her this, but I should."

"Calley, I learned more about you today than ever. It's good stuff. Did you notice my truck?"

"Are you talking about the blue Tacoma?"

"Yes, what did you think of it?"

"It's the shit. I want a black one. I am saving my money for a Tacoma and a camper."

"Damn, Calley we have a lot in common."

"I was afraid that we would."

"Don't worry girl, this can be a good thing."

Dakota and I hiked. We kept pace with one another. We talked, and we laughed.

At the end of the hike, I said "I am going to go get some vegan enchiladas at the Mexican restaurant."

"I will join you."

I really want to go by myself but decided to go with him.

"Did you hear me say vegan?"

"I did, and I am not vegan, but I have been experimenting with it and I feel like I have more energy when I eat this way."

"That is exactly how I feel and that is what helped me to become vegan. I also love animals too much to eat them."

"That is also a problem for me. Animals are incredible and I do not want to eat them. Maybe you can teach me more about the vegan lifestyle."

I smile and say, "Yes, I can hook you up with the vegan world."

We are eating our vegan enchiladas and our conversation goes deeper than I would have imagined. I am not a talker, but I felt comfortable with Dakota.

"Do you have a dog?" I ask him.

"I had a dog named Chance. Chance was a pure bread Australian shepherd. She died at age 10."

"Oh, that's young. I am sorry to hear this."

"Me too, she was my baby. I buried her in my parents' backyard. Sometimes, I think she can hear me when I lay on the ground where she is buried and talk to her. Other times, I think that's crazy. Either way, it gives me peace, so I keep talking to her. She died from seizures. I am not sure what caused the seizures. The vet does not know either. I held her in my arms as she died. For days after her death, I thought I might die too from a broken heart. I also thought about getting another dog. I've been looking but have not found one that is the right one yet. I can easily hook up my camper to my truck and have a dog travel with me for work. I would like that. I want to take my time and find the dog or maybe the dog will find me."

"I also want to take my dog, Sundance on the road with me. Sundance loves to travel so I think it would work out. She is a rescue dog and I trained her from when she was a puppy. She is a good dog. Sometimes I think all I need is my dog."

"I can relate to what you are saying Calley, but you also need love. You are going to want someone to go through life with. It's better that way. Two is better than one."

"I know people say that Dakota, but I don't know if that's true for me. I feel like someone will pull me down. There's a lot of travel and stuff I want to do in my life. I want to do it my way."

"I get what you're saying but if you find the right person, life can be really beautiful. My parents taught me that and showed me that. Now that they are older, they can lean on one another."

"That's beautiful. The other thing is I do not know if I want kids. If I have kids, my partner can't be white. I want dark kids who look like both parents. I love my mom and I love my dad, but it is hard to have one parent that is white and one that is dark. I learned a lot from it but want something different for my kids, if I ever have kids."

"I feel you on that Calley and I also want my kids to have two dark parents. I think I want kids, but I also want to live my life and travel."

"Yeah, I love to travel too. It was good to sit down with you, eat and talk."

"I never thought you would. You kept blowing me off. Why was today different Calley?"

"You caught me off guard. I built time into my trip so that I could explore some places on my way back to the job. You happened to be at one of the places I wanted to explore. What are the odds? I was going try to escape but you saw me and then I also had on the hiking boots you sent me which I slay in. There was no turning back."

"Those might be the best words I have heard out of your mouth since I met you."

"Which words?"

"The ones where you said there was no turning back."

Calley feels another smile lighting up her face. "I also learned so much about you. I'm glad we did this today."

"I learned a lot about you too."

"I do have a question though; do you know anything about being Native American?"

Dakota laughs out loud. "That is a damn good question. I know who I am, and I know what my white parents have taught me. I have Native American friends who taught me also. So, based on all of this, the answer is yes. Do I wish I knew more? Sure, but these are the cards that life dealt me, and I am good with that."

"Did you ever notice that there are not that many people of color in the na-tional parks or on the hiking trails? There are also not many people of color who are vegan?"

"I have noticed all of this Calley. Are you going to change the world and make a difference?"

"I might try, but not at this moment cause I am working on saving for a truck and stuff."

"You know girl, you can ride in my truck anytime you want."

"I know, but you know, I'm going to get my own."

"As stubborn as your ass is, I know you will have a truck."

I feel another smile coming on.

We head out and say good night. My thoughts are all jumbled. *That dang fine man. Why did I have to run into him? Then, there is this other thought, but it was nice, wasn't it? I answer myself, girl, you know it was good.*

Please Help Me!

Dru is staring at one of her favorite pictures of her husband. When he was alive, she barely looked at this picture. Now that he is gone, she finds herself gazing at it every day. She never would have envisioned this life for herself. Is this fair? Should she kill herself and make it all go away? Her pain is deep, and she has not received any therapy, so she has no relief. If she killed herself, what about her son, Hope, and what about Calley, and the kids at her school? She loves all of them so much. She so enjoys being around them. She cannot kill herself and doesn't even know how to do this. What if she tried and it did not succeed? Constant thoughts go through her mind.

She finds a new kind of happiness when she is around Cornelius. Is this right? Is she allowed to feel this joy? No, she must suffer because her husband died. She has no right to go on and find any type of joy. Cornelius is handsome, political and she would like to date him. Yet, she cannot bring herself to allow this. She wanders around home. This is the weekend, so she is not working. She looks at her husband's shoes, his jacket, pants. Where are you? she screams to a home that is empty and no response comes. How many times has she done this? Hundreds of times and never a response. She did get rid of most of his clothing, but she still keeps some of her favorite clothes around. Why? What if he comes back? He will need something to wear. Can you come back from the dead? Most people say no, but others say in spirit some can come back. What if there is a heaven, and one day she will see him again? Her head hurts from all of this thinking. She should take an aspirin, but she will just let the headache go away on its own. She hates to take pills.

A car pulls up to her driveway. It is a parent from her school with her two kids. She is excited that someone is coming to visit. She runs to the front door to greet everyone. The kids are so special to her. Maybe this day will get better. She just needs people around. This must be her dead husband's doing. He knows that she is sad and is sending friends to visit her. She looks at his picture which is near the door and quietly mumbles thank you and I love you.

After her friend and the kids leave, Dru does some of her everyday weekend things. She walks to her local shopping center where she goes to various thrift shops or the library. She remembers when her husband would drive her here or sometimes meet her at this location. When he first passed, she used to look for his van. It has now been seven years and she has not seen his van.

He was sick when he died. He had been sick for a long time. He could still move around but it took a lot of effort. He could no longer sleep at night. He was too uncomfortable. His sleep became reversed. He was up at night and tried to sleep during the day. This was hard but he was still a daily presence in her life. He would still put a blanket on her at night and tuck her in bed. They said I love you to one another. They still fought over stupid things from time-to-time. When he died, it was unexpected and in a hospital. Was there more she could have done?

She enters the local library and Cornelius is there. He is leading a political presentation. She joins the group of people that are listening, and he waves hello to her. He is a fantastic activist and a great speaker. After his presentation, she gets ready to go.

"Dru, do you want to get a cup of coffee?" he asks.

"Sure, that would be nice".

They walk to the coffee shop. He is spirited and inspired by his latest political event. He walks in long strides, and he is happy. Dru walks in slower strides. Her brown hair frames her face. Her trim figure is noticeable in the black pants she has on. Her eyes are tired from lack of sleep. She talks politics with Cornelius and enjoys the conversation. After their long discussion about politics, she asks him about his wife.

"My wife was remarkable. She could cook, sing, was an activist, a great mother, and the love of my life. Her death was expected and toward the end she suffered greatly. After she passed, I was not sure I wanted to go on. Slowly, it was the little things that brought me back. The sunrise would still come up in the mornings and I could still drink my coffee. My kids needed me. My grandkids needed me. My activism must go on. I still think of my wife every day. I go to her grave site frequently. I have her pictures in my home. I miss her, but she is not coming back. I am 71 years old and if I am lucky, I will live another 20 years or so.

When you think of how much time, I have left, it will go in the blink of an eye."

"I never in my wildest dreams, thought I would be interested in a white woman. Then I met you and this changed. It's ironic how life can be. I miss having someone to drink coffee with, to dance with or to spend time with. My wife would want me to be happy. She would want me to go on and live what life I've got left. Dru, do you want to go on?"

"There is a part of me that does and a part of me that doesn't."

"Yes, I can see that. You are getting very thin, and I am not sure that you are sleeping."

"I'm not sleeping and sometimes, I do not feel like eating much."

"Dru, I see a therapist since my wife died and this has really helped me. I talk to the therapist once a month."

"I feel like a therapist would be an intruder on my life."

"A therapist is someone that listens to you and gives suggestions You only share what you want to share. You can do it over the phone or in person. The beauty of the therapist is that they do not know you or anyone in your life. It is completely confidential."

"I don't want to take any medication."

"Why do you feel this way? "

"I am against medication."

"Well, I can tell you that when I started taking medication. It really helped me. It rounded out my emotions. I can sleep at night. I can be happy. Sure, I am sad, but not all the time. I believe in good mental health. If I had not seen my doctor and then gotten a referral to a therapist, I do not think I would have gotten to this place."

"I will have to think about this, but maybe I should try this too. I am so sad all of the time. Any joy that I used to have has left my soul."

"I can see this, and it bothers me. I knew you and your husband from before he died from the political events you attended. You have become a shell of the woman you were. It's very difficult to lose someone. Unfortunately, this is the cycle of life. Most folks don't discuss it, probably because it is so hard. Is there anything I can do to help you?"

"Just talking to me like this is helping me. I really appreciate you and admire you."

"Keep in mind I live close by, and you can always come to my home."

"Yes, I know and thank you."

Dru heads home. She will clean her house from top to bottom. This helps her to get rid of some of her anxiety and boredom when she gets home. She thinks about Cornelius. Yes, she is very much attracted to him. She still is struggling with whether it is ok to feel this way about anyone other than her husband.

Dru is thinking about so much anymore. There is a loved one in Hope's family going through a major medical scare. Why is there so much turmoil everywhere? What can she do to stop it? Is the answer just to be there for everyone and provide as much support and love as humanly possible? How do you give this support when you are hurting so deeply inside? She wants to do so much for everyone, but her own grief is overwhelming her.

She calls out to her husband, "Please help me. I need you!" There is no response which causes her to feel isolated and scared.

Maybe, it is time to seek professional help. She has been so strong-willed her entire life. She has always busiest herself with kids, work, friends, and her husband. Life is becoming much quieter as she ages. There are bones in her body that did not used to hurt, that hurt now. She cannot walk as fast as she used to. She misses so much of her old life that she is not sure she can accept her new life. She has been trying for seven years and it keeps getting more difficult. If she had a magic horse, she would ride away to a fairytale land. She looks for the magic horse and realizes there is not one waiting.

Dru takes out a piece of paper and crayons. She draws a magic horse in a fairytale land. She does find some comfort in this. In the drawing, she controls what the horse does. The horse is vivid. She colors the horse in purple and pink colors. The fairytale land is colored as a bright blue sky and green grass. Dru places the completed picture in a journal. She has been keeping a journal since her husband died. She writes to him each day. This also eases the pain in a tiny way.

Dru Meets Faith

Dru gets ready to take her walk. It is late at night, but the walking relaxes her. Her son does not know how late or dark it is at night when she walks. The walk is familiar to her, and it is part of her routine. She has never felt in danger when walking. If something happened, well that was just meant to be. She tells herself she no longer is afraid to die.

She takes her walk and for the first time, something is different. The moon is incredibly bright, and she can see very clearly. There is a woman that she passes on the sidewalk who stops her. The woman is probably the same age as Dru, she has silver hair and dark eyes which are almond shaped. She is short in stature, but her words are powerful.

"Hello, why are you out so late?"

Dru is shocked that a stranger would ask her this question, but she responds, "My husband died, and I need to walk so that I can tire my body in effort to sleep. Why are you out at this hour?"

"I never had a husband or kids. I wanted them but it never worked out. I never met my soulmate. I have not been feeling well and went to the doctor. I have bone cancer and will die in a matter of months. The funny thing is I have learned to love my life. I read, I sew, I sing, and I volunteer for various organizations. Most of my friends are dead and my parents died many years ago. Yet, I still like to get up in the mornings and have my tea and do the things I have always done. I am not ready to go."

Dru is beside herself with grief.

"I have a great family, friends, a job I like and no health problems that I know of. I am so sorry for what you are going through. I wish I could make it go away."

The stranger responds, "Thank you for your kind words. You cannot make it go away. It's life. I will see my doctor soon and get some pills to help me sleep. You should be grateful for your life, for the time you had with your husband, your family."

"I am grateful, I just am struggling to want to live."

"This is very common after you lose someone, but you must seek help and get your hormones balanced so that you can live out your best life. How long were you married?"

"I was married for 55 years."

"That is longer than a lot of people and look at me, I wanted marriage more than anything but never found it."

"What is your name?" Dru inquires.

"My name is Faith."

"My name is Dru, and it was a pleasure to meet you. I hope you live longer than what the doctors told you."

"I do too, and I hope you stop feeling sorry for yourself and start living."

"I have never run into anyone on my late-night walks that has bothered to talk to me. I am exhausted with what you have shared with me. I am going to turn around and go home and lay down. I feel different. Almost as though someone sent you to me so that I could fully grasp my own situation. Thank you, Faith."

"Dru, if you make changes to your life, it will be the greatest gift you can give yourself."

"I now realize this Faith, and I appreciate your words of wisdom."

Dru collapses in her bed when she gets home. She is fortunate. It is time to go on with the life she has left. It is the first time she has said this in seven years. She will reach out to Cornelius in the morning for a therapist's name.

Dru awakes in the morning and feels renewed. Was it the fact that Faith, a complete stranger who was not ready to die, but yet is dying, gives Dru the will to want to live? Yes, she believes it was. She calls Cornelius and he gives her the name of a female therapist. It is not his therapist, but he has heard good things about her. He asks Dru, what changed her mind.

"I met a woman who was dying. She was not ready to die, but her bone cancer will take her life in months. It was her story that caused me to question everything. I want to talk to a therapist."

"Dru, this is a huge and good step for you. I am proud of you."

The therapist calls Dru immediately after Dru completes the intake form.

"Dru, I am glad you reached out to me. I see that you have never sought therapy and you are now 71 years old. I have to admit your intake form raised a lot of red flags which is why I called you immediately. We may never meet. We can do this over the phone, if you would like. I do not know you or your family other than what you tell me. I can be your sounding board. Everything is confidential. Please share with me whatever you would like."

"I miss my husband and want to die on most days. I want my old life back. I met a woman on my walk late at night that made me feel very selfish. Her name is Faith, and she has bone cancer. She will die in a matter of months. She never married or had kids but wanted this more than anything. However, she learned to accept her life and actually love it. She is not ready to die. She told me how fortunate I was to have my family, friends, good health, and a job I love. I also was married to my husband for 55 years." Dru is now crying, "I know I am fortunate. I just do not know how to go on without my husband."

"Dru, everyone unfortunately dies at some point in life. This is very difficult. The reality is life is unpredictable and there is no guarantee. I think Faith was right when she made those comments to you. Do you go on late night walks?" " I do because I need the exercise. It helps me to clear my head."

"Can you go somewhat earlier in the day? It is very dangerous to be out there late at night."

"I could but just have not cared if something happens to me."

"It sounds like your husband was an amazing man. Tell me about him."

Dru talks about her husband for an hour. She continues to sob uncontrollably.

The therapist says, "How do you feel after talking to me for over an hour?" "Well, I do not know you. I can see your face on my phone, so it was nice to see a face. I liked not having to come into the office. I feel some relief."

"Would you video chat with me again?"

"Yes, I would. I never thought I would say this, I really need help."

"Let's talk in one week."

"I would like this. Thank you for listening to me today."

Dru feels lighter. She has shared things with a stranger. She could see her face. The therapist could see her face. It was almost as if they were in the room together. She talked about so many things. This therapist does not know her or anyone around her. It was surprisingly fulfilling.

Dru gets a cup of coffee and turns on her radio. She listens to some music and smiles. When is the last time she has smiled on her own? She cannot remember. The smile comes with tears, but the tears do no hurt as much as they usually do.

She looks at the picture of her husband and tells him, "I miss and love you, but I may choose to go on with my life. I think I want to live for the first time since your death." She wants to scream, "Where are you?" but something inside holds her back. She begins to dance to the music.

Cornelius calls Dru on the phone. "How did therapy go? "

"I never thought I would say this, but good. I liked talking to someone who I did not know. I feel lighter, like some internal weight has been lifted off of me."

Cornelius chuckles, "That's because it has. You can't hold it all in Dru. I read a quote the other day that I liked by Michael Altshuler and want to share it with you, "The bad news is that time flies. The good news is that you are the pilot."

Dakota

Dakota is done with a long day of work. He did not see Calley at work today. They do not always see one another. He has not seen or talked to her since the hike they did and the dinner they shared. He really enjoyed the time with her. It's been ten days since he last saw her, but who's counting. He is and damn it, he has never counted days before when it came to a girl.

This girl is different. His parents always thought he would never meet a girl because of his work and the travel it involves. He would love for them to meet Calley, but who knows if that will happen? She is fiercely independent and seems satisfied with her life. She doesn't need him. He doesn't need her either, but he would like a soulmate and she seems to fit the type of girl he would like. He never dreamed he would find her, but here she is. What's her name mean anyway. He looks it up on his phone, the name Calley means beautiful or lovely. Yeah, that's her. She is gorgeous and her body is pumping.

Calley, Calley he repeats to himself. He thinks about her some more. It has been a lengthy day at work. Today was a ten-hour day. He is at the campsite and is laying on his cot. *I wish I could get this girl out of my head!*

Dakota thinks about what she had on that day they hiked. She wore Nike sweatpants, a red shirt and a matching Arizona national park cap. Her dark hair was in a ponytail. She is an amazing hiker. He is also a fantastic hiker, but there were times where he struggled to keep up with her. He never struggled to keep up with anyone on the trails. This was a first! She knows every bird, every animal, the types of trees. He could go on and on. This girl blew his mind.

Dakota calls home. "Hi Mom, I'm doing good. Yes, I actually met a girl. She is a park ranger, but this is the first time we hung out. We hiked and had some vegan enchiladas. She is vegan. What's she look like? Her mom is white, and her dad is from Guyana. She is beautiful. Her name is Calley. I know you want to meet her; I don't know if I can make that happen. She is headstrong. I will let you know if it happens. I love you too."

Dakota hangs up the phone. His parents would love Calley. They have always supported everything he does. He does not know what he would do without them. They are good people who deeply love him.

He lays down and looks at some pictures of rescue dogs at the local shelter. He has been thinking about getting a dog again. He does not have time to train a puppy due to his work schedule. Perhaps, he could get a dog around 3 years old. He would get a female dog. He prefers the temperament of the female dogs, and he also finds them fiercely loyal. So many cute dogs. Maybe Calley would go to the local shelter and help him pick out a dog. Now, that's the best thought he has had all day. Now he just has to figure out how to approach her about this. She's tough so he has to plan this right. He drifts off to sleep with pictures of dogs swirl-ing in his head and the possibility of another day spent with Calley.

Dakota Goes to the Humane Society

Dakota heads to the local shelter. He did not see Calley at work earlier today and feels uncomfortable calling her. Unfortunately, they do not always see one another at work. Oh well, the dogs will take his mind off of her. The shelter is a nice size and there are a lot of dogs. He looks around and wishes he could take all of the dogs with him. He wants a dog that looks different from his dog, Chance. No one can replace Chance. He sees a dog that is in its kennel playing with someone. He walks up to the kennel.

"HI Calley, are you getting a dog too?"

"Hi Dakota, no I just come here to play with the dogs from time to time. I miss my Sundance. I don't need another dog. It just helps to fill in the time until I can bring Sundance with me."

"I want to look at the dogs. I loved my dog, Chance but now she's gone, and I think I am ready to try another dog. They are the best companions. They always love you and don't judge you."

"That is how I feel about dogs too. Just wished they lived longer lives. "

"Have you eaten yet?"

"No, do you want to go and eat something?"

"Sure, do you want to meet my friend first? This is Lily, the brown pitbull. She is sweet."

"She sure is. How often do you visit her?"

"I am here about twice a week to play with her."

"That's awesome! You are making her world so much brighter."

"Since we both drove here, do you want to meet me at the Mexican restaurant?" Dakota inquires.

"How about I drive us both in your truck?"

"Yes, that's fine."

Calley gets behind the wheel and Dakota notices her grace and ease with driving. She is a great driver. She looks good behind the wheel.

"I like the pickup on this truck and all the extras," Calley comments.

"Same with me" says Dakota and he smiles. Calley notices that he has a beautiful smile. She can't figure out how she missed that feature before. This is one man that she could really fall for. Should she? She has been so guarded for so long. She didn't want anything to interrupt her planned path for her life. Now she wonders, do we really get to plan our life, or does it just happen? How did she meet someone like Dakota? He is so different from most young men.

"So, what did you want to be when you grew up?" Dakota asks.

"I played with so many thoughts, I love cars and thought I would do something in that field. I wanted to own my own business or be a veterinarian. I do like being a park ranger but when I was younger, would have never dreamt of this. I changed as I got older. Some of my friends had kids and stuff. I also realized how much I like to travel. What about you?"

Dakota laughs and Calley catches a glimpse of that incredible smile again.

Dakota says, "Man, I wanted to rule the world. I wanted to drive a Mustang, have a bunch of side chicks, and run my own business. Don't ask what that business would be because I never figured it out. I thought about owning storage lockers and renting those out, operating a laundromat. It was the kind of businesses where I would not have to be there all the time. I started hiking with my parents and all of that stupid stuff went out the window. There is no place like the mountains. I love nature. I don't care so much about shopping or having the best of everything. I like to be in shape, to challenge myself and to be outdoors. I could never do a 9-5 job or a sit-down job. That's not me. I don't think that's you either Calley."

"Definitely, not me. We have some similarities, more than I have ever had with anyone. How did we get here?"

"I am not sure, but I am glad we did. How about you?"

"I can't lie. I am glad we did too. What do we do now?"

"I could think of a lot of things, but I am just going to start with why don't we hang out from time to time and get to know one another?"

"No, I am not ready for this!"

"Girl, you were born ready."

Calley laughs and says "Alright, let's hang out sometimes, but don't get in my way."

Dakota says "I would like nothing better than to be in your way every day, but I will take this slow seeing as I have no choice. I would rather get to know you on your terms."

"I'm good with that."

"I knew you would be and one more thing, you can take full control of setting up whatever we do."

"You must think I am a control freak."

"I don't think this, I know this!"

"Ok, you right. I am and you just made me one happy girl."

"I aim to please especially someone that looks as fine as you!"

"Well, damn, that is a nice comment coming from your fine ass. And ok, I will set up a plan for us. Here is my plan in three days we will meet back at the shelter, and I will help you pick out a dog. We will need to spend a long time at the shelter so that I can observe all the dogs."

"I agree, it's a big deal. Why do I have to wait three days to see you again?"

"I need three days to calm down. I am used to being on my own. Does this make sense?"

"Yes, it does to me. I also am used to being on my own. I have never met anyone like you Calley. I am feeling like we met for a reason. What do you think?"

"I feel like we did too, never thought I would say this, but our connection is deep. I am glad we got to know each other more and will hook up again soon."

"I am too. Thanks for bringing your beautiful, crazy ass into my life. Calley, do you know that your name means beautiful?"

"Of course, my mom told me that's why she named me Calley. She has always told me that I was beautiful and could do anything."

"Wow, your mom said all that. She sounds cool."

"She is cool, and she truly never cared about the color of my dad's skin. She loved who she loved and did not care what the world thought. She has told me this many times, wanted to make sure I understood this."

"So, do you? "

"Yes, I love my mom and I talk to her almost every day. I also love my dad. I just sometimes wish they would have thought more before the two of them got together and created me. It's not always easy to be biracial. There have been many times in my life where I felt different from everyone else. The struggle has been real."

"I have gone through this too cause like I told you both of my parents are white. I never knew my real parents. Maybe we can make some good out of this."

Calley asks, "Like what?"

"We could take a kid of color on a hike and show him or her the mountains. You know how most kids of color don't go hiking."

"Yes, I have always wanted to do this."

Calley says, "I think I know just the kid too. I will introduce you to this kid soon."

Dakota Meets Darius

"Hi Cal-Cal!" Darius hollers as she enters one of her favorite co-ops.

"Hi Darius, what up?"

Calley and Darius banter back and forth about their favorite hip hop and rap artists for a while. Darius is African American. He is 18 years old. He wears his hair in a low fade. He always has the latest shoes, the latest name brand baggy jeans and a basketball jersey. He is a huge basketball fan of several teams. Calley also loves basketball. It is yet another topic for them to banter over.

"Darius, do you want to take a hike with me and my friend?"

"You got a boyfriend now?"

Calley smiles and says, "I didn't want one, but Dakota could be that man."

"Dakota, what kind of name is that?"

"He is Native American and fine as hell. His birth parents named him Dakota, but he never knew them. He was adopted."

"For real, well, any man is a lucky man to get a girl like you."

"What's that supposed to mean?"

"You know, you are smart, pretty, brown skinned, vegan, like cars, basketball and shoes."

"Yeah, I do like all that. Remember how I have been telling you about the mountains all over this state?"

"You mean the mountains that I have only seen from a distance?"

"Yes, do you want to go hiking today? I will buy you some hiking shoes and I will pick up some hiking clothes for you. You just need to bring a backpack with some food and water. You in little man?"

"Yes, you keep talking to me about the mountains. I've never been hiking, and

I know you can save me if anything goes wrong."

"Darius, you are fit, and you eat healthy. You will be fine on this hike. What's stopped you from doing this before?"

"Cal-Cal, it's usually just white folks. I didn't know I could hike in the mountains."

"I'm about to school you, Darius. Are you in?"

"Yes, I am not working today. I stopped in to get my schedule so you got me, and I can go."

"Darius, I will meet you back here in two hours. I cannot wait to show you what you have been missing!"

Later that afternoon, Calley is driving Dakota's truck. Dakota is happy and on the passenger side. Darius gets in the backseat. Calley is blasting the rap music and is very content. She has planned out the whole trip and is in her "boss" mode. Dakota and Darius are getting along easily, as Calley expected. The hiking trail she planned out will take two hours. It is Darius's first time and she wanted to take it easy on him. She wants him to enjoy it.

Darius is looking out the truck window with wide eyes. He does not know much about nature other than what Calley shares with him when she stops in the co-op. Now that they are getting close to one of the trails, he can visualize the beauty of the sky, the terrains, and the walking trail. He feels excitement running through his body. It is strange because this is going to be great exercise which he loves, but you can chart your own course and you could see amazing animals along the way.

"Calley, this view is dope. There are no shopping malls and not many people, but the air is fresh, and the sky is blue. It's quiet but I feel like I can breathe."

"Darius, I think that you are really going to like this." Calley says.

Dakota nods his head, "It's the best, man. It's like a hidden treasure."

It is late afternoon, and the sun is breathtaking. There are less people on the trails, and she loves the quiet and also feels that it is a better time to see the animal life. She parks the truck, and they begin their hike. The weather is brisk. Calley leads the hike, Darius is in the middle and Dakota is in the back. Darius is talkative. He asks many questions. Sometimes, Calley answers and other times Dakota answers.

After the hike, Darius smiles, "I loved it and would do it again!"

"We would love to take you again" says Dakota.

"Thank you for introducing me to something that I never thought about it. It really opened my eyes. Nature is cool and hiking is cool. I also feel different." comments Darius.

"Those are all good signs. Now, we will drop you off. We are headed to the humane society tomorrow morning," Calley reveals.

"You getting a puppy Cal-Cal?"

"No, Dakota is looking at a dog, maybe three or four years old."

"Isn't your dog at home, four years old?"

"Yes, Sundance is four. You have a good memory."

"You talk about her all the time."

"I know that's my baby."

Darius gets ready to exit the truck.

"Bye Cal-Cal. Bye Dakota. It was good to meet you. You got it all in Cal-Cal."

"Bye Darius. 'See you again soon, and yes, I know Calley is it. I never thought I would meet a girl like her."

"You all stay together. You're good for one another."

"How do you know Darius?" Calley inquires.

"I see the way you all look at one another. His skin color is mocha and yours is like caramel Cal-Cal. You look good together girl."

"Thanks Darius, I will see you soon."

Calley turns and looks at Dakota, she smiles, "Good hike."

"It was a good hike and Darius liked it. He will do it again."

"Maybe we can open the mountains to kids of color by doing what we did today repeatedly with other boys and girls."

"See Calley, you are someone who wants to change the world and so do I. Are you starting to see how two are better than one? "

"Dakota, I have been "one" for a long time. I loved how Darius looked to you and me for guidance today. I cannot make promises, but I sure as hell can try to change."

"Maybe this note that Darius gave me will inspire you."

"What note?" Calley grabs Dakota's hands and uncrumples a bright yellow sticky note, which reads *Dakota-you got to have a lot of patience with a girl like Cal-Cal. She ain't easy, but bro, you can do this! Thanks for the hike and I'm gonna hit you up soon!*

A Day Off Work for Calley and Dakota

The shelter is not busy when they arrive in the morning.

"I will show you the dog I have my eye on," says Dakota.

He leads Calley to the kennel where Star is. Star is about 3 years old. She is a mix of retriever, and shepherd. Her coloring is a soft brown. Her eyes are dark. She has floppy ears and a long tail.

"Dang, she reminds me of my Sundance a little. Have you played with her yet?"

"Yes, I have."

"Is she playful?"

"Yes, she likes to fetch the ball, she can sit on command, and she seems to be very loyal."

"Let's take her in the play yard and spend some time with her so you can get to know her even better. We don't have to work today so we got nothing but time."

Star seems to like being outside. She runs around the yard. She is friendly. She barks when she wants the ball thrown. She does fetch it and bring it back.

"Why would anyone get rid of this dog?" Calley asks.

"The sign said the family was unable to continue to care for her."

"That's rough. Maybe they had small kids and could not do a dog too."

"Yeah, that could be. You never know" says Dakota.

Star whimpers when Dakota and Calley get ready to leave.

"It's so hard to leave her." says Dakota.

"Do you think she is the one?" Calley questions.

"I do, but I want to come out here a few more times and mess around with her before I make that decision."

"That makes sense. She is a good dog. If you take your time, you'll be able to feel her out more."

"That's what I was thinking, just hope no one else grabs her up. "

"I was thinking about stopping at the co-op to get some food. Do you want to come?"

"I would love to come. Is it the co-op where Darius works?"

"That is the one." says Calley with a smile.

Calley shows Dakota around the co-op.

"I really like this chickpea wrap. It is protein packed and very filling. Do you want to try one?"

"I'm in. Hey, look there is Darius."

Darius is talking to a friend of his, Athena. Athena is tall, long legged, African American woman with curly hair. Her face is round, her eyes are bright, and she has a beautiful smile. She also works at the co-op.

"Hey Darius, what up?" Dakota shouts.

"Hi, I was telling Athena about the hike. She has never been on a hike either, but she would like to go with us. I was telling her how much I liked it."

"You can both come with us next time we go." Calley beams.

Athena smiles too and introduces herself to Dakota. She already knows Calley from the co-op. Athena says, "Darius was telling me that the hike was eye opening to him. He didn't know that nature could be so deep."

"It really can be deep and beautiful." nods Calley.

Calley and Dakota say goodbye to Darius and Athena.

"Dakota, I am going to head back to the campsite. I really enjoyed the day with you. I will drive us back to my van."

"Calley, can I get a kiss?"

"No, I'm not ready to go there yet. I would definitely another day like this though."

"It was a good day. That's ok if you are not ready for a kiss yet. We can take this slow." Dakota smiles.

Calley says, "Maybe next time we will just have sex and skip the kiss."

"Girl, you are a trip. That's why I like you. You are so different from the norm."

Calley says, "I hate the norm. It's dull and boring to me."

"I feel that way too."

"Have a good night, Dakota."

"You too Calley and I hope to see you soon."

"You will, says Calley with a smile. Dakota notices she has one dimple. He had not noticed this before. He really is blown away by her natural beauty.

Brad

Brad is at his mom's house. She called him early in the morning which was unusual. He was concerned and drove over to check on her.

"Brad, I felt like your dad was right here. My dream was vivid. I could see your dad's green eyes so clearly. I could feel his thick gray hair. He put the blanket on me to make sure I was warm. I felt like I slept in bed with him all night. It was a peaceful sleep. When I looked for him this morning, he was gone."

Dru's eyes are drenched with tears. "Why he is gone, why did he leave me? Do you know I always looked at your dad as heroic? I never stopped seeing him as the young, handsome man that he was when we got married. I know he put on weight over the years and had health issues, but I always saw him as a prince. I guess I idolized him."

"Mom, dad could not have really been here. He passed away. It has now been seven years since his death. I think that you wanted him back so much that you had a very vivid dream about him. It's ok to talk about him and miss him. I do not think he could have really been here last night, other than maybe in spirit. I know that you idolized dad. I don't think this was good. I think it comes from your difficult childhood. You lost your dad and your mom remarried someone who was quite verbally abusive to you and your siblings. You didn't really get to be a child. It's dangerous to love dad as much as you did because you are falling apart without him. It is good to have some independence and to be your own person. I want to help you."

"Do you think his spirit could come back each night? "Dru sobs.

"No, mom. I think you should call the therapist and see if she can fit you in today. I think it is very important to talk about this. You can talk to me about it, but I think someone who doesn't know you directly and who is a professional would be a better way to go."

"What about Hope, could I talk to her about this?"

"Of course, you can talk to Hope, but because the therapist specializes in this, she is probably the best person to talk with. You like the therapist, right?"

"Yes, I do like her. I just feel this is too personal."

"Yes, mom I understand, but you have already talked to the therapist about dad, and it is ok to keep doing this. Do you want me to stay in the house with you while you call her?"

"Yes, that would be helpful. You don't have to listen to my conversation but then at least when I am done talking to her, I will know that you are there. It will be reassuring."

Brad goes to his old bedroom. He has many memories from this house. The memories grip him. He remembers how his dad was never there for him. His dad struggled with fatherhood. His dad's dad had struggled with it as well and this is probably where it came from. He always wanted so much more from his dad. He wanted his dad to take him to baseball games, to teach him how to drive, to tell him about being a man. His dad could never do these things. He learned from his friend's dads how to drive. He went to baseball games with friends. He learned on his own how to become a man. He even sometimes secretly wished his friend's dads were his own dad. He knew his mom had a very different view of his dad. His mom felt his dad was a hero. His dad had even become more of a hero to his mom now that he had passed. His mom was so sad; he had decided to keep the peace and never to say anything negative about his dad. Afterall, his mom had a right to remember his dad the way she wanted. He did not want to take this away from her.

As he sits in his old room, he thinks about so many things. He married Hope later in life. He was already 40 when they married. She had Calley and neither of them wanted to have another child due to their ages. He loves Calley, but he wishes she would call him more now that she has left home. She calls her mom every day. He has always known that she loves her mom. He knows that she loves him too but craves for her to reach out to him. Being a stepparent is hard. He was there for so many events in her life. He remembers all of them. Does she? Maybe he is overthinking his role as a stepdad. Calley loves her real dad. She has always been close to him, even though he was in another state. Maybe he should call Calley more often instead of waiting for her calls.

Should he have had his own kids? He has thought about that over the years. He was engaged to someone else when he was younger and at that time, they did not want kids. They both later called off the engagement. He feels like he made the right decision about his own kids. It wasn't in the cards for him.

What would his mom do right now without him? It's a good thing she had a kid. She needs him to survive his dad's death. It's funny how everyone is so different. He hears his mom coming into his old bedroom.

"How did it go mom?"

"It was helpful. I was able to cry and tell the therapist about my dream. I explained to her that it felt so real, and I was so sad when I woke up and your dad was not really here."

Dru's brown hair is in her face. Her eyes are wet with moisture. She is beside herself with internal grief that you can visually see on the exterior. She sits by Brad and hugs him.

"I love you, but I miss your dad so much! The therapist did say that I should try to focus more on the concrete things in my life, like my job, my kid, my friends. She said I should not write to your dad every day in my journal because it seems to make things harder for me. She also said I should join a therapy group for widows."

"I agree with a lot of what she said. Are you ready to join a group?"

"I would like to bounce my thoughts off you. You knew your dad and loved him like me."

"I think it would be better for you to meet with others who have gone through this process. They could relate to you better. "

Dru cries more, and Brad holds her in his arms.

"I just miss Denny so much and I wish he was still here. Why did he leave me? Why does death have to happen? We had a good life. I miss my life the way it used to be!"

"Ma, I understand that you miss dad. This is the cycle of life. In truth, it is very short and goes fast. You had many great years with dad. He is not coming back. His body was falling part and he was sick. You have me, Hope, Calley, friends, and your job. We all are here for you. You are making progress with the therapist. You also have Cornelius who really likes you."

"I know and I appreciate everyone. I like Cornelius too, but if I were ever to date, wouldn't that be cheating on your dad?"

"No, dad is not here mom, and it would not be cheating. Hope and I have talked about down the road if one of us goes first, either of us can date again. We want each other to live happy lives. It is ok to think this way. "

"Thanks for being here for me honey, it means the world to me. Brad, are you upset with me? Do you think I am over the top with things?" Dru is sobbing again.

"No mom, I am not upset. I just wish you could go on with your life. Dad is unfortunately not coming back. Enjoy what time you have left of life. Do you want to have dinner tonight with Hope and me? If you would like, Cornelius could come?"

"Yes, maybe I could do that later tonight. Let me get back to you on this and thank you for asking."

"Yes, of course, I want to help mom in any way I can."

"I know you do honey."

"Mom, what if we take a trip soon to see Calley? What if we go hiking in the mountains? I think it would be good for you to get away. Calley always says she loves the way the mountains take her mind off of everything."

"I have never done this Brad, but I would love to see Calley, and I would love to go."

"I know Hope has been wanting to go as well. We can talk more about it tonight at dinner. "

"Thanks Brad, I love you."

"I love you too mom."

Dru watches Brad drive away. She cries more. She looks at herself in the mirror. Her eyes are drained. Her face is pale. There are so many days when she no longer recognizes the woman she has become since Denny died. Maybe she should take a bath, do her hair, and put something nice on. She could also call Cornelius.

"I have nothing to lose anymore!" she screams to an empty room. She then picks up the phone and dials Cornelius.

"Hi, would you like to come to dinner tonight at my son's house?"

"Hi Dru, yes, I would. Thank you for calling."

"Thank you for picking up the phone and for being willing to come."

Dru hangs up the phone. She talks out loud to herself. *I cannot keep crying. I must try to live amongst the living. I will not make it if I do not try. I must try.* She is not sure where the power of these words came from today. Perhaps it is a combination of so many things.

"Yes, my mom is coming over for dinner with Cornelius tonight", Brad tells Hope on his cell phone as he drives home.

"Good, I'm glad she is bringing Cornelius. This is a big move for her in the right direction."

"Well, I told her to bring him. She had a dream where she felt my dad was with her and then she woke up and realized he wasn't there. She cried for hours. She did call her therapist which seemed to help. I talked to her and told her it is time to try to move on and live out the years she has left."

"Yes, I agree, she really needs to try to do this. I will make vegan chili, asparagus, and vegan cornbread."

"That sounds great. I hope all goes well tonight."

"Yes, me too."

A Table Set for Four

The table is set for four and thankfully, there are four people. Dru did come with Cornelius. Hope looks at Dru. She has on a black shirt, blue jeans, and a blue jean jacket. Her brown hair is pulled back in a ponytail. A small barrette with beads holds her hair in place. She has no makeup on which is not unusual. She never wears makeup. She has on a small necklace with a silver heart, small earrings, and the rings she has worn for many years. Her eyes look tired but there is a small spark of joy within them. Dru is also getting very thin, but this has been going on since Denny died. Overall, Dru looks better today than Hope has seen her look in a while. Hope glances at Cornelius. He has on a blue and gray plaid shirt, white t-shirt underneath, and blue jeans. He has his hair in braids but pulled back in a po-nytail. He is a handsome man. Hope can see that he is concerned about Dru but is trying to be optimistic. She glances at Brad who seems content. His dark brown hair neatly frames his face. He has on a gray sweatshirt and jeans. His dark eyes scan the room and meet Hope's eyes. They smile a private smile. Hope has on jeans, a pink hoodie and her hair is styled the same as usual, bangs, and a longer bob cut.

"Cornelius, welcome to our home. I am so glad you could come". says Brad.

"I am glad to be here too," smiles Cornelius.

Sugar and Sundance run into the kitchen. They are already familiar with Dru and give her kisses. They smell Cornelius and decide they love him. He also gets kisses.

"Beautiful, well-behaved dogs." Cornelius comments.

"Calley trained them. Her favorite is Sundance, but she loves Sugar too. She has spent more time with Sundance. She rescued both dogs. Sundance was rescued in Florida and Sugar is a rescue from Arizona." explains Hope.

"I think Calley can do anything. She is one smart girl" says Cornelius.

"We think so too." says Brad with a grin.

Brad looks at his mom who seems content and perplexed at the same time. He is sure that she is worried that she is cheating on his dad. He smiles at his mom, and she lightly smiles back at him.

"Cornelius, tell me about your wife, Dorothy."

"Dorothy was a spectacular woman and I loved her completely. She was my soulmate. We did political events together, cooked together, danced together, and loved our life. I miss her, but I cannot bring her back. We lived a great life. I keep pictures up of her throughout our home. I try to keep her memory alive every day by talking to her as I look at her picture. She would want me to go on with my life."

"I think that is good and a very healthy way to look at your life." remarks Brad.

"I think so too Brad, but I didn't get to this place right away. It took time and counseling. I also miss having someone in my life to share it with."

"This all makes sense Cornelius. Thanks for sharing this with us."

"How is the food?" inquires Hope.

"We are really enjoying it honey, "says Dru.

"I am so glad to hear this." beams Hope.

They listen to jazz records after dinner and relax.

"We have been thinking about going to Arizona and visiting Calley. We would go hiking in the mountains. Calley would be our guide. Would you be interested in going Cornelius?" Brad inquires.

"Yes, I would love to go! I love to hike and there is nothing like a majestic mountain. What about you Dru? Would you go?"

"I have never hiked in the mountains, and I am scared." says Dru with tears in her eyes.

"Mom, Hope and I have never hiked in the mountains either, but Calley has, and she will guide us."

"Well, Calley is one of my most favorite people in the world. I would love to go as I have to see my granddaughter!"

Cornelius says, "You know Dru, I have hiked in the mountains many times with my kids and my wife. I can also be a guide. My family used to go on a trip almost every year to a different state where we always hiked in the mountains. There is something surreal about the fresh mountain air and the beautiful views as you hike at a high elevation. We can take the hike slow because this is new to all of you."

"It sounds like you and your family had so many precious memories," comments Hope.

"We did. I sometimes wish I could go back in time, but I cannot. I had an issue with my foot about a month ago. It hurt me when I walked. I was afraid that I would never hike again. I did go see my doctor and I have arthritis, but it is treatable. I will be able to hike again. When Dorothy was around, I never worried because I knew she would take care of me. When I had this pain in my foot, I was scared and now that I live alone, I had a hard time getting to the doctor."

"I am glad your foot is ok. I know it is hard for my mom to live alone too, especially when for so many years she had someone there, "says Brad.

"It really is hard Brad. The other thing I do lately is I think harder about getting a new appliance because, the appliance may be under warranty for the next ten years, but I do not know if I will be here. I would rather put the money away for my kids than put it into an appliance. I also hesitate to get another dog or cat because what if I am not here when the animal needs me? The only thing I am sure about is a relationship, because we could both take care of one another. Dru and I are about the same age. We would have each other until we didn't. No pressure on Dru. I know she doesn't know if she wants another relationship. This is just how I look at the world."

Brad comments, "Hope and I have been thinking a lot about things as we get older. If one of us goes first, we want the other one to go on and date. I guess it is similar to what you are describing Cornelius. It's funny because I married late in life, but I am glad I did. I also become a stepdad which was both hard and good in so many ways. I was so used to my independence and now I have become dependent on Hope in some ways. Life is such a crazy thing. You do really have to make the most of it."

"Why did you wait so long to get married Brad?" Cornelius asks.

"I dated a lot of girls and was even engaged to someone else at one point. It just didn't work out. Most of the girls I dated wanted much more than I could give them materialistically or wanted to control my life. I did not want to deal with either one of these things, so I would end the relationships. When Hope and I met, she didn't ask for much. I was grateful. Does this make sense?"

"It makes a lot of sense Brad. Dorothy never put pressure on me which is why I married her at a young age and was very happy. We met while I was visiting Jamaica. She was working at one of the fruit stands and we got to talking. I loved her simplicity and her zest for life. She eventually came to the United States, and we married. I have been to Jamaica many times though. "

"That's another place that Hope and I wish to visit at some point. We really want to travel and to enjoy the outdoors. You know that Calley taught herself how to hike in the mountains. She plans out her trips, drives to the destination and maps everything out."

"Calley really is ambitious. I wish I had been more like her when I was young," comments Hope. She is also driven and disciplined."

"Yes, I have noticed that she is really something." nods Cornelius. "Tell me more about the hiking trip, Brad."

"Calley and her friend Dakota, would meet us at the airport in Arizona. Dakota has a camper. Calley also wants to take Sundance on the trip so we could take Sundance with us on the flight. She has taken Sundance hiking before. Calley has mapped out the hiking areas and says she made sure the trails were easy. She called me last night to discuss it. It's funny I always wish she would call me more often and then she called last night, and we spoke for a while. She calls her mom every day and sometimes I feel very left out, but last night was awesome! Hope and I are thrilled to go on this trip. Mom, how are you feeling?"

"I am looking forward to some different scenery. Maybe it will be good for me to get away."

"I think it will, Mom. It's good to try new things."

"You know since your dad died, I have tried to do familiar things, but nothing takes away the pain and maybe nothing ever will. You're right about trying something totally different. I have nothing to lose anymore," says Dru tearfully.

Cornelius pats Dru's hand. "Dru, please try to believe that life can still be good. You are alive and healthy. There are many people that wish they aged well and have mobility."

"You're right Cornelius, I will try to see a positive side. I am just struggling and have been now for years since Denny's death."

"I know Dru, I know. Just remember I am here for you. Sometimes life gives you a second chance. Brad, I am going to drive your mom home. I look forward to going on the trip with you soon. Hope, thanks for the lovely meal."

"You're welcome, it was our pleasure." says Hope.

Calley and Dakota

Calley glances at Dakota and takes in his strong cheekbones and handsome side profile. "Are you nervous about meeting my mom's side of the family? You will meet my mom, stepdad, my grandma Dru and Cornelius, my grandma's friend, and my dog, Sundance!"

"Actually, I am shocked that you are asking me to meet your family. Yes, hell yeah, I want to meet them. I think this is cool about doing a hiking trip. I am also excited to meet your dog, Sundance. Are you good with Sundance coming on the plane?"

"Yeah, Sundance is a tough dog. She will be able to handle the plane ride. She might be a little scared but when she sees me, she will be good. She knows I will protect her and that I am her owner. She will be happy."

"It's nice that I have access to a large RV that my parents have used when they visit me. This RV will work perfect for your family. The camper would have been tight quarters"

Calley remarks, "I love this RV. There is so much space and it is going to be good for fitting everyone in. Thank you, Dakota!"

"You got it Calley, anytime. You know I would do anything for you girl."

"Anything?" Calley says with mischievous smile.

Dakota nods, "Yes, anything." He takes in her beauty again as he looks at her in the passenger side of his truck. For once, she has let him drive. Her hair is down. It is thick, wavy, it frames her brown skinned face. Her face is a piece of art. It's as though someone sculpted her eyes, her nose, and her full mouth. She is incredible looking, and the best part is, she doesn't even realize it. She is such a tomboy, and it is rare for her hair to be down. It's always up in a ponytail. Her hair is thick and incredible. He feels like he could self-destruct with the beauty that Calley radiates.

They have arrived at the airport. Calley sees her mom and family. She runs to greet them. It is Sundance that she is most concerned about. Sundance gives Calley a hug. She has always known how to hug Calley. It is an adorable thing to watch. Sundance gets up and puts her paws around Calley and showers her with kisses.

Hope smiles. "Hi Calley, Sundance did good."

"Hi mom, and yes, she did good. I was worried."

"I know baby. I was too."

Dakota takes in each person. Hope is shorter than Calley. He can see some of Calley's features in Hope. Hope is attractive and has the dimples. Her hair is dark brown with red highlights. She dresses casually but stylish. Brad is the stepdad. He had dark brown hair, is in shape and seems easy to get along with. Dakota re-members Calley saying they are vegan and like to work out. Dru seems sad like she lost someone and lost herself. He knows from Calley that she lost her husband. Dru is also attractive but very slim. Cornelius is hip. He has braids in a ponytail and dresses in a way that really suits him, a plaid shirt, blue jeans, and combat boots. Dakota feels comfortable in this group. He sees that Calley is happy to have them here.

Hope whispers to Brad, "Dakota is so handsome. Calley never looked happier. I know Dakota is in love and I think Calley may be too. I am so glad to be in Ari-zona and so excited to see Calley and get to know Dakota better. "

Dru gives Calley a hug and whispers, "Dakota is so good-looking baby doll. I knew he would be, but he looks like a movie star. And you look beautiful."

"Thanks grandma. I am happy."

Next Brad and Hope embrace Calley.

Dakota and Cornelius are talking about the RV and the size of it, how well it drives, and hiking. Their conversation is easy and natural. They are comfortable with one another.

Calley takes in the surroundings and smiles. Sundance is at her side, "I think this is going to be a great trip." Sundance goes to sniff Dakota, and he passes the test. Soon Sundance is giving him kisses.

"I can see why you missed Sundance so much Calley." She is magnificent, and so loyal to you."

"She is the best dog." agrees Calley.

Hope approaches Dakota and gives him a hug. "It's a pleasure to meet you. My daughter is everything to me. She is my most prized possession. I was hoping she would stay near me, but she wanted to travel."

"Hi Hope, it's good to meet you. I can see some of Calley in you. She has showed me pictures of her dad, so I know where the other half of her comes from. Yes, your daughter loves travel, the outdoors, and she is a skilled hiker. I have never met such as stubborn, beautiful, girl. I feel very lucky!"

Hope, laughs, and Dakota notices her dimples. Her smile is similar to Calley's.

"Cal has always been stubborn. I think it comes from when her dad and I split. It is really hard on a child. We also lived in two separate states. I lived in Iowa and Calley's dad in Florida. Calley had all of my family who doted on her, but no one replaced her dad. I did not realize the impact this had on her until I became older. Cal still saw her dad, but she needed him right there by her as she was growing up. Also, because Calley is biracial, she needed to see that other half of her family on a daily basis."

Dakota smiles and realizes that Hope is so easy to talk to. "You know that both of my parents are white. I was adopted. I never met my real parents. I never felt the need. I love my adoptive parents, but there were many days where I looked for others that looked like me. I am now at a phase in my life, where I do not need to do this, but I do remember those days. Hiking was my survival method. When I hike, I escape everything. Anyway, I can see why Calley is your most prized possession. If she chooses to date me, she would be mine too. I have never felt the way I feel about Calley with any other girl."

"She has not decided to date you yet?" Hope questions. She looks over at her daughter who is engaged in a conversation with Brad, Cornelius and Dru. Calley's hair is up in a ponytail. She has on her Arizona national park t-shirt, a state park cap, and black sweatpants. She has on a new pair of Adidas tennis shoes. She is dressed so casually but the way she puts together the clothing, suits her and looks good on her. How could anyone not love this girl? She is everything.

Dakota says, "No, she wants to take it slow. She is used to being independent."

"This is all very true. I do know from my conversations with Calley that she really likes you. She thinks you are unlike most men and enjoys the time she spends with you."

"That is good to hear. Thanks for sharing that with me. I am not giving up on her. Rather, I am waiting for her. I am not a patient man. I have never waited for anything. I really haven't even dated a whole lot. It's not my thing. The land is my thing. I enjoy the work I do. Calley would be the first girl I have ever waited for and that is because I feel she is more than worth the wait."

Hope smiles and shakes her head. "Calley is the total package and is worth the wait. I cannot say enough good things about my daughter. She is the person I picture in my head every day. I talk to her every day. I think about her every day. I only had one kid, but I guess I kind of worship her in a sense. I am so proud of the person she is and the skills she has."

"Yes, I can see that you are." says Dakota with a grin.

Calley comes over with Dru, Brad and Cornelius. "Mom, we will need to eat and get some rest. We will hike an easy trail in the morning. The RV is spacious enough for all of us to sleep."

Hope responds, "Calley, I am so excited to hike and be in the mountains! I am so happy to be near you and Dakota. This is my dream trip."

"Mom, I think you will love the mountains. I picked out some easy trails for all of us. It will be peaceful. Grandma Dru needs a place to find peace."

"Yes, she does Cal."

The sunrise comes early in the morning. Everyone is up. Calley is explaining that we should not eat too heavy. We can eat a light breakfast. She has provided everyone with protein bars, water, and small snacks for their backpacks. The sunrise is majestic. Everyone is in good spirits.

Calley drives the RV away from the campground and off to the designated hiking path.

Dru is content. She loves her granddaughter and is delighted to be on a trip with her. She thinks Dakota is gorgeous and they make a beautiful couple. Cornelius is sitting next to her, but they are still in the friendship phase and may be there forever. She does enjoy him, and she is glad he is on the trip with her. He gets along so easily with her family. What a blessing!

Cornelius is happy. He loves the warm weather and the mountains. He is glad he came, and he notices something different with Dru. She is more relaxed. Maybe the hiking in the mountains will do her a lot of good.

Hope is sitting next to Brad and is excited. She now sees why her daughter loves the mountains. There is nothing like it. She is eager to hike and see more.

Brad feels total contentment. He is pleased with the trip planning that Calley did. The RV is working out great. He is ready to see the mountains and the surroundings. He is glad his mom came with Cornelius.

Dakota feels inner peace. He likes Calley's family. He admires Cornelius who is an old man, but hip, political and deep. He can now see the love that Calley's family has for her. One of the coolest things is the bond between Calley and Sundance. Sundance got up on her hind legs and hugged Calley and kissed her.

Sundance is quite possessive over Calley. Sundance watches Dakota carefully. Sundance likes him but her love for Calley is fierce. Sundance is now in the front of the RV laying at the side of Calley's seat as she drives. Sundance wanted to go on Calley's lap, but Calley was able to get her to lay down by the side of the driver's seat. Sundance just lays there with a smile on her face. As long as she can see Calley, she is content. Dakota smirks to himself and tells his inner soul, *I guess I am like Sundance when it comes to Calley.*

"This is the trail!" Calley announces with excitement. Calley and Sundance lead. Dru and Cornelius follow, Brad and Hope are next, with Dakota at the back of the trail. The weather is the low 70s. The view is spectacular with views of the canyons, mountains, and organ pipe cactus.

Calley goes at an easy pace so that the others can follow. Hope and Brad share a smile. This is just the kind of trip they needed.

"I wonder if we should think about moving out here?" says Hope.

"It is a possibility. I must admit, I really love the mountains," Brad comments.

"It would be a very different life for us as we age, but also a good one," comments Hope.

"I agree, definitely something to think about. Let's enjoy our time here and explore all that Calley has put together!"

After an hour into the hike, everyone seems to be holding up. Calley views the group from the front and Dakota from the back. There is one more hour to go and this is the only hike for today. Dakota walks up to Calley to talk to her about the last hour. As they are talking, Dru slips and is falling on the trail. Cornelius quickly grabs her and makes sure she is ok.

"Yes, I am fine. Thank you for saving me. I think I am not used to the altitude yet."

"The altitude effects everyone differently nods Cornelius. Some thrive in it and others take time to adjust."

"Grandma are you ok?" yells Calley from the front.

"Yes, honey, I just need to get used to the altitude."

"You will come to love it. It just takes time. We can stop hiking for today." We will just walk back slowly and take pictures as we head back.

"That sounds great Cal. says Brad. Taking pictures of nature is one of my favorite things."

"You may see a variety of birds and other wildlife in this area." says Dakota.

Dru looks at Cornelius and says "Thank you for keeping me upright on the trail. I appreciate you looking out for me."

"I was happy to help you. I did not want anything to happen to you. Sometimes I think about the days when Dorothy was still alive. I never thought I would be in this situation. Always thought I would have my Dorothy to walk through the golden years with me."

"I can relate to that. I also thought I would always have Denny to walk through these years with me. I do not think of them as golden. Why did they ever call them that? These are the years where you lose so many people, where your kids begin to get diagnosed with different ailments. Your body isn't as strong as it used to be. The list goes on and on. For the life of me, I cannot figure out what is golden about it!"

Cornelius laughs heartily, which makes his dreadlocks shake.

"I think they call it golden because its whatever you make of it. Some folks can retire and still have their other half to spend it with. The problem is that at some point, one of them is going to go. That's life and the other one has to figure out how to spend his or her life without that person. How to keep alive those memories, how to start over again if they choose to."

"Being out here near the mountains and fresh air really makes me think. says Dru. I am not busy at work. I cannot escape and go shopping. My mind just thinks. It really is hard to know how to preserve the life of your loved one and keep the memories alive. So many times, I wished I was the one who died. It would have been easier."

"Easier for you Dru?"

"Yes, because I would not have to figure out how to go on without Denny."

"Do you think when he died in the hospital, it was pain free and easy for him?"

"No, I don't Cornelius. I think it was hard. I think he suffered greatly."

"Dorothy also suffered significantly. I had to let her go as I knew how much pain she was in. I knew she did not want to go on like that. There was no quality of life left. We are lucky at our ages, to be walking on this trail right now. There are others that would not be able to do this."

Dru nods and thinks about what Cornelius said. She thinks about not being able to walk and how incredibly difficult that would be.

Dakota looks at Sundance and comments to Calley, "She isn't even tired. She could hike for hours, and she has a smile on her face."

"I know says Calley, that's why she is my dog. She's my girl."

"Now that I see Sundance, I do not know if I want to get Star. I want a dog just like Sundance."

"Take your time, the right dog will come to you. Sundance came to me. I rescued her in a hurricane in Florida."

"Yeah, you're right Calley. You're always right."

"Dakota, I have something for you. Here you go." Calley plants a kiss on his lips.

"That was the best part of my hike today!"

"Mine too!"

Hope and Brad notice the interaction between Dakota and Calley. Hope smiles and says "They are perfect for one another! I really like Dakota."

"I do too," says Brad. "He is one hell of a guy. I trust him completely with Cal."

Hope says, "I do too Brad. I want things to work out with them. Imagine what beautiful grandbabies we would have!"

"Hope, you know that Cal may not want kids. She has told you that. She wants to be free to travel."

"Yes, I know, and I want her to be able to live her life the way she desires. If they were to have kids, they would be amazing! It's ok for me to wish, but I will accept whatever Calley chooses because that is what moms do."

Brad takes Hope's hand and says, "Good babe, that is the right attitude."

Sundance walks up by each member of her family and kisses them. Calley has her off leash and Sundance is checking on everyone.

"All good Sundance?" asks Calley. Sundance smiles and barks. She then runs up to Calley and gives her a hug.

"Can I get a hug Sundance?" Sundance sniffs Dakota and looks at him with her head tilted sideways as if questioning him. Dakota roars with laughter.

Calley remarks, "You're a trip Sundance, you know that?"

Sundance runs back to Calley and stays close to her. Her love for Calley defies everything. Sundance loves Calley without speaking. She shows Calley her love as only a dog can. Calley also communicates this to Sundance by her actions, including the extra belly rubs, checking her paws after the hike to make sure she is not hurt, and giving her a stuffed animal or her favorite treat.

Calley puts Sundance on a leash and hands her to Brad.

"I am going to jog down the trail and get the RV."

As Calley begins to jog, Sundance barks. Calley turns around.

"I will be back Sundance, you wait." Calley starts to jog again, and she hears Sundance howling. She runs back to her. Sundance has her head up and is howling. This goes on for minutes. Calley has tears in her eyes. Hope is trying to comfort Sundance, but no one can.

"Mom, you told me Sundance howled before one time when I left, but this I the first time I am seeing it. It's incredible and heartbreaking."

"Calley, it means she needs you and is vocalizing that she doesn't want to be without you." says Dakota.

Calley puts her arms around Sundance and Sundance melts in her arms. She showers Calley with hugs and kisses.

"Calley, she doesn't want you to leave her anymore, comments Hope through tears. As much as we love her, you're her everything."

"I don't have my truck and trailer yet. That's the only reason I have not taken her yet."

"I have a truck and trailer where Sundance can stay, if you want her to remain in Arizona." Dakota says while wiping tears out of his eyes.

"You would let her stay in your trailer?"

"Of course, Calley, I would do anything for you and for your dog."

"I don't think I have a choice. Sundance has spoken loud and clear. I cannot leave her any longer. I'm sorry Sundance that I caused you pain. You will stay with me now."

"We are going to miss her so much says Hope and Brad nods. She is the dog that we cuddle with, walk with, talk to, bathe. She is Sugar's partner."

"You are the love of her life." Dru says "I will miss the kisses she always gives me, so much affection as if she knows my inner soul is hurting."

"She does know grandma. She can sense it. I cannot live without her or her without me. Sugar will be ok. "

"As hard as this is Calley, you have made the right choice." says Brad.

Calley says, "Sundance you can jog down the trail with me to get the RV. You will see me every day from now on."

Sundance hugs Calley and they jog down the trail together. It is a beautiful vision. Sundance's beautiful black and brown coloring, her ears flapping, her long tail flying and a smile on her face. Calley's dark, thick hair is in a ponytail, her athletic figure running next to Sundance. Their stride is the same, a smile on both faces. Calley, Brad, Dakota, Dru and Cornelius are in tears.

Dakota asks Hope, "So you have seen Sundance howl before?"

"Yes, it was the first time Calley left. Calley had shut the door and said goodbye. Sundance howled for a long time. I should have captured it on my phone, but I was stunned and was busy trying to comfort Sundance."

"Sundance's love for Calley is pure and simple. It is unconditional and surpasses all boundaries. Calley has a way with animals, and I am an animal lover, so I have the utmost respect for that." Dakota explains.

"That is so kind of you to let Calley use your truck and trailer until she gets her own. Thank you." comments Hope.

"Hope, I fell in love with your daughter quite some time ago. I do not want to scare her off, so I am keeping my mouth shut. Between you and me, I would do anything for her. She is a prize."

"I am so happy that you found one another, and I can see she loves you, she is afraid to express this to you. Please give her time."

"I will!, I will!" nods Dakota.

Dakota and Calley are discussing Star with everyone in the RV. Dakota mentions, "Star is the dog that I thought I might want to adopt at the humane society. She is a great dog, but I do not think she is the dog for me. I had a dog named Chance that I loved, and I know I cannot replace her, but I want to keep looking. Now that Sundance is staying with us, could you take a dog with you on your flight home?"

Brad nods his head in agreement, "Calley is very much into rescuing dogs. We live in an old farmhouse and have land. Sugar will need another partner. Let's go to the shelter and see Star."

"Look at this, Star has been adopted and is gone!" exclaims Dakota.

"She was a good dog, and I am not surprised says Calley. Let's see what other dogs are here today. "

"Check this out Cal, this dog's name is Mountain." says Hope. "Why do you think someone would name the dog Mountain?"

"I know why I would. I would name the dog Mountain because I love the mountains!" says Calley.

"Do you think it is as simple as that?"

"I do mom, life can be that simple. The profile says that the family had to move and could no longer take care of Mountain."

"That is always sad to read and must be distressing for the family." Cornelius explains.

"Yes, I agree," says Dru. "Giving up a dog that you love is difficult." Mountain has an interesting gray color with dark spots. Her dark eyes are deep and tell their own story. "What does it say for the breed?"

Dakota says, "It says unknown. Let's take her in the yard to get to know her."

The yard at this humane society is spacious and inviting. Mountain trots along with Calley's family. Dakota tosses a ball to her, and she sniffs it. Calley laughs, she does not like to play ball. Calley tosses a frisbee which gets the same reaction by Mountain.

Calley says, "There are nice trails, let's take Mountain on them and see if she likes to walk. She responds well to her name. Her age is three years old."

"Calley, we will wait in the yard while you and Dakota take Mountain on the trails, "says Hope.

"Ok mom, see you soon!"

Mountain likes to walk, and she seems to be able to keep up with Calley and Dakota. She is a sweet dog with an easy disposition.

"I think she would be a good fit with Sugar." exclaims Calley. "I would love to save her. I get such a thrill out of saving a dog. I feel like I have done something good for the world."

"That is because you have. A dog needs love, another dog if possible and people. Everyone needs someone that they belong to or feel a connection to. I think we should take Mountain out a couple more times before we make a decision for your family to take her back on the plane."

"Yes, I agree. They still have more vacation time with us so there is not a huge hurry. We can stop by again and get a better feel for Mountain."

"I like the name Mountain, "says Hope. "I read some more on her profile. It says it was a young couple with a baby who moved to Arizona to be near the mountains. That is why they picked her name. The husband is sick with cancer and the family cannot afford to care for her at this time."

"That's a sad story. You hear stories like this too often." comments Cornelius. Dru is crying over the story. "Dru, you have to believe that life is not always sad. There is good stuff too. Like this vacation and the fact that Calley and Dakota will probably save Mountain." Dru wipes her tears and nods her head as Cornelius speaks.

Sundance and Mountain

Calley adopts Mountain and leaves the humane society with her at her side. As she approaches the RV, she calls Sundance who instantly comes to Calley.

"Sundance, this is your new friend, Mountain."

Sundance snorts and sniffs Mountain up and down.

"Hello Mountain. Calley is my master. I love her and I will need you to keep your distance. Calley takes good care of me. I know her family. She gives me tummy rubs, bathes me when I am dirty, checks my paws to make sure I am not injured after a hike. She takes me to dog parks. She lets me ride with the windows open. I get peanut butter from time to time. She gives me the best dog food and treats. I also like that she is of color, like me. Do you feel me, Mountain?"

"Look Sundance, I can see why you love Calley. I wish she was my master too. She told me I will be going back to Iowa, and I will get to play in a big yard with another dog, named Sugar. I am glad to be free and going to a good home. I have been through a lot with my previous family. They loved me, but the dad got sick and then they could not care for me. The humane society is not the life that I want for myself."

"Ok Mountain, then we are good. I am glad Calley saved you. You will like Sugar. As for me, I need my Calley and now I finally get to have her with me all the time. I will have to learn to like Dakota. I know he is a good guy, and I can see that he loves Calley. I don't want to share her, but maybe he will not be around all the time."

"Just think how lucky you are to be with Calley all the time. Most dogs don't get that life. Do you like to hike?"

"I love to hike. I like exploring. I can check out the different scents in the air,

I am always trying to catch an animal, I like breathing the outside air, and drinking fresh water. What about you?"

"My first family named me Mountain because they loved the mountains. I like to hike but I am also lazy. I could lay in a yard all day and be content."

"That is how Sugar is so you will be in good company. Just don't take her toys. She is possessive over her toys. I am sure Hope will buy you your own toys. Hope will take you through the aisles at the pet store and let you pick what you want."

"I have never gotten to do that. I would like that! My previous family loved me but became so busy. Maybe Hope, Brad and Sugar will have more time for me. I dream of laying on the couch and them petting me or snuggling up in bed with them. I hope Sugar and I can become close. I want a family!"

"Hope and Brad are wonderful people and they always treated me with love. I will miss them, but because Calley is their daughter, I will always see them. Sugar is good too. I think you will have the family you want. We can become friends. Welcome to my family Mountain!"

"Thank you, Sundance, for making my world a better place and for welcoming me into your world! Can we shake paws on this?"

Sundance and Mountain shake paws and trot alongside one another.

Calley and Dakota are watching the interaction between Sundance and Mountain intently. Calley has noticed the way they tilt their heads, and their barks seem to be a conversation. She watches Sundance with so much love. Sundance has always amazed her. She almost feels like Sundance just put Mountain in her place. Could this be? They are just dogs. No, there so much more than dogs. They are highly intelligent and fascinating creatures.

Calley looks at Dakota and remarks, "They just had a conversation about us and now they are friends."

Dakota smiles at Calley and says "Babe, you are right."

Sundance runs up to Calley and gives her a hug. Calley gives Sundance a hug back.

"Did you have a good conversation with Mountain?" Sundance tilts her head. She is listening to Calley. She smiles and barks with a nod. Calley strokes Sundance and kisses her on her head.

"I love you Sundance and I need you."

Mountain comes up to Calley and gives her a kiss and then goes to Dakota and gives him a kiss. Mountain than proceeds to get acquainted with Cornelius, Dru, Hope and Brad. Sundance watches while being embraced by Calley.

"Calley, you made a good choice. I think Mountain is going to get along well with Sugar. It seems as though Mountain and Sundance have an understanding," says Hope.

"I think so too mom. They seemed to be communicating. It was thrilling to watch."

"I can also see how happy Sundance is in your presence. She loves you unconditionally just as you love her."

Calley smiles and remarks "I have missed her so much and it is wonderful to have her with me now. She is my hiker, my hugger, my passenger in the van, my everything. I will make room for Dakota too."

Hope gives Calley a hug and responds "It's time Cal to let a man into your life. Dakota is a good man. He will always protect you and fight for you. He cares very deeply for you."

"I know mom and I care deeply for him. I just don't know how to show it."

"The same way you show love to Sundance is the same way you can convey it to Dakota."

Dakota is close by and can hear the conversation. He pretends he is busy and cannot hear it. He glances at Hope, makes eye contact and whispers "Thank you."

Trip Over

Hope's eyes are misty, and she reveals to Brad, "I wish we had more time. We leave today. I really enjoyed the mountains and getting away from the world. It was refreshing."

"I know, it was a great trip. I have some incredible pictures of the birds, and various animals we saw during our hikes. I also took some nice pictures of all of us. It's always good to have pictures as they capture memories."

Dakota joins Brad and Hope. "I know I will see you both again. It was a pleasure to meet you. Now, when I hear stories, I can put the names with the faces."

"It was our pleasure to meet you. Come visit us anytime or if easier, we can make more trips to you, Calley and Sundance," says Hope.

"We will figure all this out mom says Calley, as she emerges with Sundance at her side. We may be in another state soon with our work, but you can always come and then you get to travel and see more."

"I loved the hiking and the trails you set up for us Cal. You did an incredible job." says Brad.

"Calley, I am going to miss my favorite granddaughter. I love watching you grow into your own person. You are so precious. Always remember this, " says Dru as she hugs Calley.

"Yes, Calley and Dakota, thank you for everything!" Cornelius adds and he hugs both of them.

Mountain watches everything and feels comfortable with this family. She is nervous about the plane ride, but Sundance has told her it will be ok and has given her tips on how to get through it. Mountain feels grateful for this new family and a new chance for a good life.

Mountain notices Hope sitting down and sees the tears in her eyes. Mountain goes over and comforts Hope. Hope hugs mountain and lets her lay on her lap. She whispers to Mountain, "Everything is going to be ok. I miss my daughter and it's always hard for me to leave. I know I have to leave but it never is easy. This is the cycle of life. They grow up and you must let them live their lives. Maybe one day, I will be in the same state as my daughter but for now, this is what it looks like, so I have to make the best of it and respect her dreams. We will take good care of you Mountain. Sugar will be good to you. You are safe." Mountain licks her hand.

Calley, Dakota and Sundance come over to Hope and Mountain. Calley kisses her mom on the top of her head.

"Mom, you know I love you. I am so glad you came, and Sundance is now with me. Thank you for taking Mountain and giving her a home. I am happy you got to meet Dakota too."

"Me too baby, me too. I am not sure what I will do without Sundance, but I know she needs you. Dakota, it has been a remarkable journey. Please take good care of my daughter as I already know you will."

Dakota says, "Of course I will, and I hope to see you soon."

"Who is picking you up at the airport mom?"

"Jade and Jaxton, Cornelius's kids, explains Hope. They are fraternal twins, and it will be nice to meet them. Grandma Dru has not met them yet either."

Dru comes over to Calley and embraces her. She whispers in Calley's ear, "You know I never feel like I see enough of you. This was a wonderful week. I love you. "

"I love you too grandma. You did a good job keeping up on the hikes. I like the way Cornelius takes care of you. I hear his kids are picking you up at the airport."

"Yes, I have never met Jade and Jaxton yet. This will be my first time. I am nervous. We are not dating but I do not know what they will think of me."

"Why grandma, because you are white?"

"Yes, that is part of it and the other part is because I am not treating their dad as great as I am sure they would like. I will never be like their mom."

"This is all true grandma, but you just got to be you. I do wish you would date Cornelius. You are not committing some terrible sin by doing this. He is a good man."

"Calley, you have a great guy too."

"I know Grandma, I am going to date him. I love the time I spend with him. I did not know that being with someone could be this good. Also, if I ever have kids, the blend of both our skins will make beautiful babies."

"Yes, the babies would be beautiful Cal." says grandma.

"What's this about babies?" inquires Hope as she hears the end of the conversation. Hope has a slight smile on her face. She has been dreaming of grandbabies and knows that Calley is not ready now for them, but just the thought that she might have them one day is exciting.

"I said I might have babies one day mom."

"This is the first time I ever heard you say that, and I am very excited!" "Don't get too excited mom. I am not sure if I want babies. I love traveling and I am not sure I can do that with a baby."

"I know Cal. Just follow you heart as you always have. The rest will come."

"You used to always tell me that, mom, and I never believed this, but for the first time, I do feel like you might be right. I feel like the stars are lining up. I am very content in my job, my life and now I have my dog too."

"To hear you say these words, makes my heart melt. I have always wanted you to have a life that you love, and I see that you have that. As much as I miss you, I accept all of your choices and I am so proud of you."

Sundance smiles and Hope smiles at Sundance.

"I am going to miss you too Sundance. You are the best dog that there ever was. I am glad you have your Calley. Watch over her for me." says Hope as she strokes Sundance's ears and kisses her head.

"You know mom, I want you to be happy too. Just because I am not in the same state as you, does not mean your life is over. Embrace your life and enjoy every minute. I may come back one day; I just do not know right now what that looks like."

"I know baby and I have begun to embrace my life. I am writing more, going out more with friends, family and with your stepdad. It is also fun to play with Sugar and now we will have Mountain too."

"Mountain will do well with Sugar. They will get along better than Sundance and Sugar. Sundance was always my dog. She just wants me. Sugar likes to have another dog around. It should work out well. I might even try to save another dog. You have enough space at the farmhouse."

"We do Calley, and I agree with you, if we can save another dog, we should. I love how you love dogs and want to make the world a better place for the ones that need a home."

Brad looks at Hope and knows she is having a tough time leaving her daughter. He knows she is trying to be strong but also knows that Calley is her ultimate weakness. She wants Calley to live in Iowa so she can see her all the time. Calley wants to travel. Brad feels that Hope needs to respect Calley's wishes. He has talked to Hope about this, and she has said she will do this. He can see she is trying to let go. Brad thinks to himself, *why is it so hard? Maybe because Calley is not my biological daughter, the feelings are different for me. I love Calley, but I am glad to see her on her own.*

Brad walks over to Calley. "Cal, make sure you give your mom a couple of hugs. She struggles when it is time to leave you."

Calley smiles, "I have hugs for everyone. It was a great trip."

Dakota grins and says "After everyone is done hugging Calley, they can hug me. I also enjoyed the trip and liked meeting all of you."

Hugs are exchanged and the acknowledgement of a trip over is apparent on the faces of each person. It is also apparent on Sundance who is the happiest she has been in a long time as she is reconnected with her soulmate. Mountain is eager to go pick out toys in a new state. Brad is ready to go home. He looks again at Hope and knows that she is not eager to go. How different they are, and yet they are couple who love one another. Dru is tearful and sorry to leave her granddaughter. Going home does not mean much to her anymore. There is no one at home waiting for her. Cornelius is ready to go meet his kids at the airport. He has missed his kids and is eager to see them. He is nervous about Dru meeting them for the first time. He is not sure how they will feel about her.

Jade and Jaxton

Jade's hair is braided on top of her head. She has her hoops in and as Jaxton glances over at her, he reflects to himself on how good looking she is. Well, he must be good looking too. They are twins after all!

"Jade, what do you think Dru looks like?"

"I don't know bro; dad didn't tell us. Mom was so beautiful that I guess I want to imagine she looks like mom. Mom could dress too. She was really amazing! That woman could cook and dance. I don't think there is anything mom could not do. I miss her every day. I am glad we still have dad, and I am grateful for the time we had with mom. Sometimes, I get angry that she is gone, but not for long because dad taught me to go forward."

"I know what you mean. I miss her too, but dad's got the right attitude. You know you look a lot like mom, and you got her style too."

"Jaxton, you are sweet and that's probably the best compliment in the world cause our mom was the shit."

Jaxton tilts his head and laughs, "Yes, she was! Are you good with dad dating?"

"Yes, I want dad to have a life and I want him to be happy."

"I want pops to be happy too. He has always been there for us."

"True that Jaxton, true that."

Jade parks her SUV at the airport and glances over at her brother in the passenger seat. He wears his hair in a low fade cut. He has on a red and blue plaid shirt, jeans and his Jordans. His features are the same as hers, smooth chocolate skin, long eyelashes, dark eyes, a broad nose, and a full mouth. They really do look like a mix of their mom and dad. Jade has always thought both of their parents were good looking, so she feels blessed that she and Jaxton resemble them.

"Jaxton, what do you think Dru looks like for real?"

"I think she is a black woman with beautiful curly hair, and a thick figure. "

"Do you think pops at his age, still looks for beautiful women?"

"Oh, hell yeah, that never ends Jade!"

"What if she is not a black woman?"

Jaxton smirks, "What you talking about Jade, dad only dates black women."

"We only know mama and they were married forever, so you don't know that."

"Ok, let's just say I would be surprised. Wouldn't you?"

"I would respect whatever choice dad makes cause I love him and want him to be his best self."

"You know you're lying Jade."

"The problem with you Jaxton is you know me too well." say Jade with a big smile.

"Do you think about Mom a lot and are you angry she is gone?" Jaxton says with tears in his eyes. Jade wipes away her brother's tears and gives him a hug.

"I think about her all the time. I am angry she is gone. I started seeing a therapist to help me deal with my anger. It is helping. I used to look around and wonder why others still had their mamas, but mine was gone. I would be trying on some clothes and see some girl with her mom. Her mom was giving her advice on which outfit looked best. I was so jealous and angry. I cannot tell you how many times mama and I went shopping. She was always there to consult me. Damn, and then when I had kids, my kids had the best grandma in the world and now she is gone. I had to hold my babies and explain to them that grandma was gone, and she was not coming back. My babies cried and cried. I sobbed too. I got to the point where I couldn't cry anymore. I had to hit rock bottom to get back up to the top. I had to breathe again to be the best mom, wife, sister, and daughter. I still see mama, but I know she is gone. I look at pictures and savor memories. I remember everything about her. I don't want to lose the memories, so I have started keeping a journal. I'm not mad anymore. Sometimes I am sad, but I know I must be strong, and I also remember the pain she was in toward the end of her life. She needed to go, and she couldn't live with the pain. Mom was a person of joy and never wanted to be a person of pain."

Jaxton and Jade are now both shedding tears and then they smile at one another. "We got each other and pops." they say in unison.

"Speaking of pops. Here he comes." says Jaxton. We better brush these tears away and put on our happy faces, "says Jade.

Jade and Jaxton exit the SUV and run to their dad. He embraces both of them with a strong hug and a fierce kiss.

"I am so glad to see my works of art and you came to the airport to pick me up. I have the best kids in the world. I want you to meet Dru, her son Brad and his wife Hope, and their new dog, Mountain."

Dru comes forward and gives Jade and Jaxton a hug. "You are both beautiful and your dad loves you so much. It is good to meet you."

"It is nice to meet you too." say Jade and Jaxton.

Mountain comes easily to Jade and Jaxton, and she likes them both. She plants kisses on them and smells them thoroughly. "I like her name." says Jaxton.

"Yes, I do also. The folks that had her, had to give her up due to the father of the family getting cancer. They also had to move out of Arizona. They moved there to be close to the mountains." explains Hope.

"We know all about cancer say Jade and Jaxton together. It took our mama also."

"Your dad told me about this, says Brad. I am so sorry your mom is no longer here. I also know what it is like to lose a parent. I lost my dad. The pain never goes away. I try to preserve the memories."

"That is what we do too. Our dad has really helped us to cope and to remember mama. We would be lost without him. He keeps us all together and keeps us strong" explain Jade and Jaxton.

"Your dad is an amazing man. What a great hiker! I could hardly keep up with him." exclaims Brad.

Jade and Jaxton nod and smile with appreciation.

"We are going to head home. It was a pleasure to meet you. We will drop Dru off at her house. Thanks, Cornelius, for making the trip. See you soon!" says Brad.

Cornelius climbs into the SUV and closes the door.

"I cannot believe Dru is white, and she is skinny pop. She doesn't look anything like I thought she would. How could you go from mama to Dru!" shouts Jade. Tears stream down her eyes.

"My beautiful Jade, Dru and I are not dating. I tried to date her, but it is not working out. I do like her family, and I do like her. I just don't get white women. I have never dated one before and I think I might be better to stick with my own kind. It's just easier. I notice when Dru and I hang out, I get these looks from white folks. I am not used to this. I don't think I want to deal with it. I do not even have to break up with her because we were not in a relationship. We can still be friends, but I am done trying to date her. I am more comfortable with a black woman by my side."

"Oh dad, I didn't mean to hurt you. I was just surprised. I hope you are not mad at me."

"No baby you could never make me mad. It's good for you to express your feelings. Do you remember when you dated that white boy, Jake?"

"Yes, daddy, I do. I did like him, but it was too hard. I always felt like I was trying to be somebody I wasn't. I married me a black man and it felt natural and right."

"Pop, we are going to love you no matter who you choose to date. Lord knows I dated a whole lot of white women. I never cared what other folks thought. It was my choice. And you both know; I don't pay no attention to what people say. I could care less." says Jaxton.

"Ain't that the truth! My girlfriends all wanted to date you and you were too busy with your white women!" laughs Jade. "Truthfully, it made me mad. I think black men should date their own kind, but when it comes to my brother, I knew I had to shut my loud ass mouth, so I did. It's just that black women have it going on."

Jaxton and Cornelius laugh and nod their heads, "You right Jade, you right."

Cornelius says, "Truthfully Jade, I want you always to see people for who they are, not by the color of their skin. For example, Dru does not have a racist bone in her body. She is always about doing good for the community. She shares my political views and has a grandchild that is biracial. I want you to believe the best in people still exists. I understand that you are very comfortable being married to a black man. I was comfortable being married to your mama. Your brother likes to date white women from time-to-time. It is ok for him to do this. Don't judge him for this."

"No daddy, I am not judging Jaxton or anyone else. I am entitled to my own views, and I feel safe when I express them to you and to Jaxon."

Life Is for the Living

His house is a modest ranch house. He has wooden floors throughout the house. The furniture is simple but well made. There are leather couches in the living room area. The goal was always to make it comfortable. There are some silk flower arrangements throughout the house. The flower arrangements are also simple, but beautiful. There are pictures of the family, jazz singers, and Jamaican artwork on the walls. The house is well organized. The paint on the walls has been well maintained over the years. The paint in the kitchen is bright orange. There are various colors throughout the home. There are modern shades that cover the windows in every room. Each shade is a different color based on the paint of the room. The exterior of the home is brick. This is his castle and is a familiarity to him. He and Dorothy raised a family here. They made love in this home, ate meals in the home, danced, laughed, and cried here.

The knock at the front door jars Cornelius out of his memories. He looks through the peep hole. He smiles wide and opens the door for his grandkids, Simone, and Antone. The fraternal twins enter the home and give their grandpop a big hug.

"Mama said you came home last night from your trip. We wanted to stop by and see you. We missed you," says Simone.

"Stop by any time you want. I love my grandkids, you know that. There is something else I want to tell you and I want you to always remember this."

"What is it grandpa?" asks Antone.

"It is simply this, life is for the living. You may have some struggles in your life. When you do, think of this phrase: Live your life and enjoy it! Even when it is not perfect, it is you who makes it good. Like today, I got up and I was thinking about some stuff. I went into my kitchen and had my cup of coffee and looked out my patio. I felt good. I like my home and I like my life."

"Sounds like words that make sense. We appreciate you sharing them with us." says Antone.

"Yes, we always think about what you tell us." explains Simone.

The three of them embrace and hold one another as the sunlight pours into the kitchen.

Cornelius looks at Antone and Simone who are now 25 years old. He remembers his only grandkids throughout the years with great memories of hiking, dancing, eating, taking them to political events, and talking to Dorothy for hours about how proud he is of his grandkids.

Jade and her husband were always meant to have kids. They are patient, loving parents. Jaxton never had kids and never married. He certainly has dated many women but is happy with his life and has not yet married. He may never marry. Cornelius and Dorothy made their peace with this a long time ago. They love Jaxton and support his decisions.

Cornelius thinks to himself, *but these grandkids! Antone with his cornrows, husky build, and beautiful facial features which are a combination of Jade and his dad. Antone dresses casual and is not big on the latest brands. He has on a sweatshirt, blue jeans, and sneakers. Simone, who looks just like her mama in her face, wears her hair in a sleek bun. She has on a simple outfit. A blue jean skirt with a matching jean top and sandals. She is long and lean.*

Cornelius looks at both grandkids with pride and inquires "Do you want my vegan waffles for breakfast? I can put some strawberries, blueberries, and walnuts on top. I have some of that maple syrup which you love."

"Yes, granddad, we want your cooking. Why do you think we stopped by around breakfast time?" laughs Simone.

Cornelius turns on jazz music. Simone and Antone sit at the wooden table and talk while Cornelius makes breakfast. Cornelius smiles to himself and reflects on the good things in life. He is a happy, lucky man.

Breakfast was great and the grandkids stayed for hours. He showed them the pictures of his recent trip. They asked about Dru, and he explained that he liked her, but she was hurting from the loss of her husband. He felt she might never recover from it. Simone and Antone hugged on him and told them how much they loved him. They left and he watched them drive away with a smile on his face.

Cornelius decided to take a walk down to his local co-op. As he checked out of the co-op, he talked as he always did to Sharon. Sharon was someone he had known for years. She enjoyed working at the co-op and her husband had died three years ago. Sharon was a beautiful black woman with a warm personality. She had a zest for life. She missed her husband but wanted to go on with the years she had left. She had known Dorothy from her shopping at the co-op and always told Cornelius what a great woman Dorothy was. Cornelius had never met Sharon's husband but from the stories that Sharon told, he felt like he had a good picture of who her husband was. He was a stand-up guy who loved his family.

The simple conversation between Sharon and Cornelius changed today. It went deeper. At the end of the conversation, Cornelius asked her out. He wanted to go dancing tonight at a local jazz club. Sharon nodded and smiled. She loved to dance. She would be delighted to join him.

As Cornelius walked home, he ran into Dru. He smiled and they gave each other a hug.

"Dru, I want to be real with you. I am coming back from the co-op, and I asked Sharon out. It was not to hurt you. I like you but you and I are not dating. Are you ok with this?"

Dru cried and explained, "I am not crying over you. I am crying because it is all I do anymore since Denny passed away. You're right. We are not dating. I am not mad. I know who Sharon is. She is beautiful. I hope you too have a good time tonight. I know you love jazz."

"You know we can still be friends; you can still stop by, and we can hang out. I wish you wouldn't be so sad all the time. I think the therapy helped you, but you may need some medicine. I can't tell you what to do, I just want the best for you."

Dru cried some more. Cornelius held her to try to console her. Her tears were dark and deep. He realized as he held her that he felt sorry for her and her pain. He was not used to a woman who was so broken. Even if he liked her, she would probably never be the woman for him. He liked strong women who wanted to live their lives. He thought about reaching out to Brad with how broken he felt Dru was. Maybe he would make that call later today.

Dru stopped crying, wiped her eyes, and apologized to Cornelius. "It's ok Dru. You needed to cry. I'm not mad at you. Where are you headed?"

"Nowhere, I am just out for a walk. I am trying to clear my head. I didn't sleep well. I never do. Usually, the walking wakes me up."

"We are right near my house. Let me drop these groceries off and I can walk with you."

"No, it's ok, I am used to walking alone. I will be alright. I just need to do it. Thank you for being my friend."

"You know you are always welcome, and I got your back. Have a good walk Dru."

Cornelius goes inside his home and calls Brad. Brad picks up on the first ring. "Hi Brad. I was walking back from the co-op and ran into your mom. She was crying a lot. I held her and tried to console her. She continued to talk about how she missed your dad. When, I left her, she had calmed down and said she was going for a walk to clear her head as she never sleeps well. The other piece I want to tell you, is that we are no longer dating. It should not come as a surprise as the dating thing never really went anywhere. I asked someone out tonight. It is a woman I have known for years. I told your mom, and she was fine with it. No one can replace her Denny and we will continue to be friends. The part I am worried about Brad, is the deep, dark sadness from within her soul. She is so unhappy. I suggested medication."

"Thanks for calling me, Cornelius. We were all rooting for you. I would have loved you as a stepdad. I appreciate you letting me know about my mom's mental status. I know it is not good. Only a man with a lot of compassion would take the time to make this phone call. You're a happy man Corn, despite the fact that your wife has passed. I wish my mom could follow suit. I guess you can't change people. You have to accept them as they are and do the best you can. Yes, she needs to be on medication, but she wouldn't take it. I cannot make her take it and I am tired of arguing with her about this. She made a mistake by letting you go. I don't think she can see this. She is too sad. Please stay in our life. Call us and come over anytime."

"Thank you, Brad. I will keep in touch with all of you including your mom. I am good at keeping in touch. I appreciate the people in my life. That's what makes me the man I am today. Life is for the living Brad. Never forget this quote. I shared this quote with my grandkids this morning."

"I like the quote Corn, and I will not forget. Thank you. What are you up to tonight?"

"I am taking Sharon dancing at the local jazz club."

"Sharon is a lucky woman. Hope and I may stop in there tonight. If we do, we will say hi."

"Sounds good Brad. Hope to see you there!"

Brad hangs up the phone and turns to Hope, "Want to go to the jazz club tonight?"

"I would love to. What is going on with your mom?"

Corn called off the dating. They are still friends. He is taking someone named Sharon out to the club tonight. My mom is too sad for him. He wants someone with a zest for life. He is deeply concerned about my mom. He suggested medication and I explained that we have been down that road. It is a road to nowhere. Damn, I would have loved Cornelius as a stepdad. I love who he is."

"I do too Brad. The good news is we will still see him. It sounds like we will see him tonight!"

As Brad and Hope enter the jazz club, Brad wipes away a tear. He spots Cornelius with Sharon. Sharon is lovely and it is easy to see that they are getting along well. Corn is not having to work at it. It is flowing naturally. Brad and Hope watch their moves on the dance floor and are envious. They can dance!

Cornelius comes over and introduces Sharon. The couples talk and listen to the jazz music for hours. Hugs are exchanged and Brad and Hope head home.

"Brad, I wish that could have been your mom in there with Corn."

"Hope, you have no idea of how much I wished the same thing. I also feel bad because I didn't call my mom. I am running out of suggestions for her. I love her, I no longer know what to do to help her. "

Mountain

Mountain greets Brad and Hope as they enter their farmhouse. She is now their greeter. Sugar does not like to greet you when you come in. She prefers to watch you enter. Hope thinks of Sundance. Sundance was an incredible greeter who would come running down from whatever room she was in to say hello. Hope misses Sundance but knows how happy Calley is to have Sundance by her side now. Mountain and Sugar get along, but still need more time to adjust to one another.

Mountain seems to like the family and to be happy. Hope reflects on the day she took Mountain to get toys at the pet store. Mountain went crazy. She picked so many toys. She smiled as she picked each toy. Mountain keeps all of her toys near her and plays with them all the time.

Hope and Brad take their dogs outside to run around in their yard. Mountain and Sugar chase one another. Once they are tired, they come inside. Hope takes time to stroke Mountain and hold her. Brad does the same with Sugar.

Mountain tells Sugar. "I am happy here. I feel loved. Thank you for letting me into your home."

Sugar responds "I miss Sundance, but she had to go. She wanted to be with Calley. I am glad you are here. I'm happy that Calley saved you. I think we can become close."

Neither Hope nor Brad stop their dogs from barking. They both feel they are communicating to one another.

Calley calls Hope on the phone and wants to know how Mountain is doing.

"She seems to be doing great Cal. Mountain and Sugar play in the yard. They chase one another until they are tired. They will not sleep next to one another yet. Their food bowls are in separate places and so are their toys. They seem to love one another but are also very cautious. They need more time together. How is Sundance doing?"

"Sundance follows me everywhere. She does not want me out of her sight. She loves Dakota but is still protective over me. Dakota and I are doing good too. We jive with one another, and it is easy mama."

"Oh, baby I'm so glad to hear this! We miss you already. We also miss Dakota and the mountains. Cornelius is dating someone named Sharon. He and your Grandma Dru are just friends."

"Grandma Dru wouldn't let him in. She is too busy thinking about Grandpa Denny who is gone. Cornelius has a different attitude. He takes life as it comes, and he makes the best of it. I am sorry that didn't work out though, I liked him," says Calley.

"You may still see him when you come home. We keep in touch with him. I liked him too and do not want to lose the friendship."

Calley says, "That's good. He is good people. I will send you some of the pictures I took of the mountains."

"I would like that. I love the perfection that your pictures capture."

"Got to go Moms, look for the pics soon."

Brad comes into the den and Hope shows him the pictures on her phone that Calley sent of the mountains.

"I loved that trip. I find the mountains to be my happy place. I can get away from everything. It is like a utopia for me. Look at these pictures of the majestic mountains, the blue sky, the cactus, the landscape! It is so breathtaking that is seems surreal. Yet, we were right there in the midst of it, hiking!"

"I feel the same way, Brad. Maybe we can move towards the mountains when we are ready. Who knows where Calley will be living by the time we relocate. Perhaps she will be in one state, and we could live by her."

"It is a possibility that this could happen. More so than ever before. I guess I needed that trip to decide. I wonder if Mountain misses the mountains. It's her namesake after all."

Hope looks at Mountain who is laying down on one side of the couch. Sugar is on the other. Mountain starts barking. The barking is focused directly on Sugar. Hope smiles, and thinks Mountain is probably telling Sugar about the mountains right now.

"Sug, I do miss the mountains. It's good for a dog to hike in that fresh air. So much to look at and do. I am happy to be here. I feel like I am loved more. I must say the mountains are amazing. I'm proud I was named after them. We will have to get you to the mountains at some point so you can see what I am talking about. "

Sugar smiles and says, "I would like that. When should we go?"

Mountain gets up, stretches, and goes into the other room. Sugar follows. "We will have to wait on whenever Brad and Hope go back to the mountains. That is where Sundance is. They have been talking a lot about the mountains, so I bet they make another trip soon."

Sugar asks, "Is Sundance happy?"

"She is beyond happy. She is with her master, Calley. Sundance is hiking a lot now, but she has done it before, and she loves it! She is like a new dog. She was happy here too, but no one makes her as happy as Calley. Sundance told me to take good care of you."

"Mountain, you have been good to me. I just need time to adjust to Sundance being gone. I miss her. I am glad I got you. I like hearing about the mountains, and I like your name. I never met a dog named Mountain before!"

"You're the first dog named Sugar that I met, but your name fits you. I see how you like treats!".

"That's true! Sundance used to tease me all the time about treats," sniffles Sugar.

"It's ok Sug, I got you," barks Mountain as she places her paws on Sugar's head.

When Lovers Hike

Calley and Dakota are holding hands as they begin their hike. Their relationship has taken leaps and bounds in ways they never knew were possible. Calley has found she enjoys Dakota's company. Instead of saying no, she has started saying yes. She cannot recall a time where she has felt more complete and happier.

Dakota is a changed man. His love for Calley is beyond any love he has ever experienced. It is pure and simple. He did not know a love like this was possible.

How did they get to this place? Neither one knows. They just let life happen and it became beautiful for them. Neither one had dated a lot of other people. Their shared love for nature, exploration, and simplicity helped to shape the couple they have become.

Dakota had wanted love from Calley right away but then he waited patiently. It was the best thing he ever did. Calley was her own person and when she felt secure, she let her guard down and gave Dakota love. She just needed time to get to know him and love him.

Sundance was ahead of both of them on the trail. She came racing back to Calley and smiled. Calley swooped her up and gave her a kiss. She then placed Sundance down on the ground. Sundance went over to Dakota and licked his hand.

Dakota stopped hiking and gave Sundance a kiss on the top of her head. He stroked her neck and her ears. Sundance happily trotted back to Calley.

"Look at this area Cal, it looks like there was once a resort here. See the guest house, the old bathroom, the fireplace, the old gas pump? There are no signs that say no trespassing. Do you want to explore?" asks Dakota.

"I would love to, and I want to take some pictures!" Calley replies.

Calley, Dakota and Sundance spend hours exploring the old resort. The mountains are nearby, the air is crisp, the cacti are everywhere. The sky is blue, and the land is vast and untouched. There are no other people out yet. This is what they like best. It is a deep shared love of what nature provides and it is theirs to enjoy and savor.

"Should we go back to the campground and grill some food?" asks Dakota.

"Yes, I am ready to eat, and I know Sundance wants some food. Let's do it."

Sundance is now familiar with the campground. She makes her rounds and says hello to the people she has met thus far. Each person gets a kiss and then she runs back to Calley's side.

Calley and Sundance embrace and then she lays by Calley's side and stares at her with complete devotion.

Dakota has black bean burgers on the grill and corn on the cob. He is playing reggae music as he grills. The campground is peaceful, and life feels good.

Dakota glances at Calley who is now laying in the hammock. Her thick hair spread out and her eyes closed. Sundance has jumped into the hammock and Calley is holding her tightly.. Calley looks so relaxed and happy.

Dakota walks over to the hammock and bends down; he puts his lips on Calley's and kisses her. "Babe, the food is ready."

Calley kisses him and rises up. "We did so much exploring. I have a lot of research to do about what we found at the abandoned resort. I am going to do that after I eat. "

"I want to help with that. I like to research. It was amazing what we discovered! We can go into my camper and go through all the pictures together."

"That sounds good Dakota. I had a great day." says Calley.

"Me too. My life feels like it is not my own anymore because I am happier and more fulfilled than I ever dreamed I could be. I feel like I am walking on air. I don't want to this to end."

"I never thought I would say this, but I feel the same way and there is no way I want something this good to end." says Calley. She hugs Dakota tightly. They both smile and begin to eat.

Sundance barks. "Oh, I better feed her now". says Calley as she gets up to get Sundance's food. Sundance follows her as Calley carefully puts a mixture of dry dog food, salmon oil and a little wet food together. She puts water out for Sundance to drink. All of Sundance's food is placed carefully near Calley's food. This is the way Sundance prefers it.

"I feel good. That was a simple dinner and really hit the spot!" says Calley.

She is laying on the cot in the camper. Her hair is loose, and she has on a black t-shirt with a national park on it. She has on sweatpants. Her feet are bare.

Dakota is laying on the cot next to her. His hair is not in its usual ponytail. It is free. It is black and thick. His eyes are half closed, and he has a smile on his face.

Calley looks at Dakota. He is so damn handsome, such strong facial features, and strong bones. His he so masculine even with his long hair. His body is muscular and thick. She leans over and kisses him. Dakota grabs Calley and kisses her back with such tenderness and passion.

Calley is now on top of Dakota. He takes in her beauty. Even her brown feet are perfect. She does not wear nail polish on her nails or feet. She has such a natural beauty that it sends shock waves through his body. He loves her natural look.

They kiss and embrace. They talk about the hike and the pictures. Dakota pulls out his phone and they research some of the pictures they took at the abandoned resort.

Sundance watches them and then when she feels the time is right, she jumps on the cot next to Calley. Dakota and Calley laugh and snuggle with Sundance. Suddenly Sundance jumps off the cot and grabs one of her toys. She brings one to Dakota. She then brings one to Calley and the last one is hers. She is now back on the cot. Each member of her family has one of her precious toys. This is very important to her. Calley and Dakota know this. They tease Sundance with the toys for a while and then the three of them fall asleep.

Calley awakes and looks into the deep dark eyes of Dakota who is gazing at her. "What are you looking at?"

"I am looking at a deep, intelligent, ambitious, young, beautiful woman."

"You can say that all day." says Calley with a grin. Dakota kisses Calley and they playfully caress one another. Sundance wakes up and jumps off the cot and lays on the ground beneath them.

"Morning Sundance!" Calley and Dakota shout. Sundance sulks on the ground. There are still times where she has to get used to someone taking away Calley's attention.

"Sundance come here. Do you want to go on a hike?" asks Calley. Sundance cocks her head. She is listening. She kisses Calley.

It is early morning and the three of them go on a hike. Sundance is now happy and is leading the hike. Calley has her hair in her ponytail. She is dressed in black sweats with a t-shirt and a national park cap on. Dakota has his hair pulled back into a ponytail. His tall frame is dressed in gray sweatpants, and he has on a dark blue t-shirt. As the hike starts out, they hold hands and talk. They point out birds, cacti, and animal footprints to one another. They talk excitingly about the trails they want to take.

Hmmm... Calley thinks to herself. This must be what hiking with a lover feels like. She breathes the air and takes in the surroundings. A big smile forms across her face. It is a smile of pure victory.

Her Name is Mona, and I Could Not Say No

She is small in size. She takes after her parents. She has long brown hair. Her hair is thin, she has a straight nose, green eyes, and a small mouth. Her skin is white, and her personality is strong, but broken. She is thirteen years old, and she lays in a bedroom at Dru's house. She is dressed in white sweatpants and a baby blue sweatshirt. She is curled up in a ball in the bed and is sleeping under the blankets.

Dru walks into the room and looks at Mona. Her heart breaks as she thinks of what this child has been through. She decides to let Mona sleep.

Dru sits down at her kitchen table and asks herself questions, that she alone will have to formulate the answers to. *Did I do the right thing by letting Mona live with me? What if something happens to Mona, who will care for her? Am I physically, and more importantly, emotionally able to care for a young girl? Will my home be better with someone else in it? Will Mona's losses help me to cope with my loss of Denny? Can we balance each other out?*

Dru cries and cries as she tries to think of the answers to these questions in her head. Her tears drip onto her kitchen table, forming a small puddle. Dru has seen more tears than this since Denny passed. Now she has a thirteen-year-old girl sleeping in her home. Mona should not see these tears, or should she? Perhaps Mona cries her own tears over her pain of losing both parents in a car crash.

Mona was twelve years old when this happened. Her parents were headed to the grocery store, and they swerved to miss a gray wolf that was in the road. The wolf lived but they did not. Their truck smashed into a tree and the impact killed them both instantly. This was when they lived in Montana. That is where Mona is from. She came to Iowa to live with her father's sister. This was not working out. Her father's sister never had kids and did not know how to raise a young girl.

It was too much for her. She had a nervous breakdown and came to the school and asked for help.

Dru has worked with Mona in the school and offered help. No one wanted to put Mona in the foster care system. This is how they got to this place…

Dru has had Mona one day. Mona came home with her Friday after school. Today is now Saturday and Mona is sleeping while Dru is thinking, but her mind is cloudy. Dru's thoughts cannot come through clearly, as she does not sleep well.

Dru hears Mona walking into the kitchen and quickly takes a napkin and wipes the tears from her face and from the table. She looks up and looks at Mona. She had nothing to fear. Mona's eyes are red, swollen and she has been crying.

"Come Mona, let me hug you."

Mona comes to Dru, and they embrace. This is the embrace of two lost souls who are looking to one another for the meaning of life and how to go on.

"Tell me Mona, why did your parents name you Mona? I like your name, but I have a feeling there is a meaning behind it. "

"There is. My parents wanted to name me Montana because they had such love for the state. They loved the mountains, the animals, and the land. My mom thought they should shorten the name and that's when they came up with Mona. I am Mona from Montana."

"That's a beautiful story Mona. Do you plan to go back to Montana?"

"I do. I have the same passion for the Montana that my parents had. I may work on a ranch. I will finish my schooling here, so I have another five years. I do not love it here, but I am here, and I know the schools are good. I miss the nature, the mountains and all the beauty that Montana has. It's different here. Thank you for taking me in. I'm sorry I was crying. I cry because of my circumstances. I am not crying for my parents. They died trying to protect a gray wolf, which was important to them. I miss them, but I know they loved me, and they were not trying to leave me. It just happened. I am strong because that's how they raised me. I just feel bad about things not working out with my dad's sister, Grace. She is a good person; she just does not want kids. It's too hard on her. "

Dru says, "I have always loved kids. I had a hard childhood and want to make a difference in a kid's life. I can help you. I may need help also. I have fallen apart since my husband died. He was my everything and now he is gone. I have my son and he is grown and has his own life and family. I do not get to see them as much as I would like. I am lonely and when I am busy, I am ok. It's when I am not busy that I break down. I can cook for you, and we can do things together if that is ok with you. "

"Dru, I would like that. Thank you again for taking me into your home."

Dru and Mona let go of one another and smile together. Dru begins to make breakfast for her and Mona. Perhaps she will begin to eat more now that Mona is here. She has not been eating much.

Mona gets out one of her books and sits at the kitchen table and reads while Dru cooks.

Dru glances at Mona as she is cooking. Mona is deep into her book. Her brown, wispy hair frames her face. She looks peaceful. Dru recognizes a fellow book lover when she sees one. Mona may be significantly younger than her, but how very cool. She has not had another book lover in her home for quite some time. It feels good to have this child in her home. It makes Dru feel like she has more of a purpose to serve as someone needs her. This is something she always felt with Denny. She has a strong desire to be needed.

She smiles silently to herself as she makes pancakes. Could this child give her a zest for life? The very life that has been taken from her when Denny passed. Not sure, but its sure worth exploring and seeing what happens. She keeps a journal. This started after Denny died. It was a way to keep Denny alive. She writes him every day. She also keeps another journal where she writes about daily things she wants to remember, which include, a day where she spent time with family, a day where someone at school said they needed her, and a day where something good in her life happened. She grabs the journal and writes today; Mona came to live with me. I am making pancakes for breakfast. Mona is reading her book with the ferocity of a book lover. *I like having someone in my kitchen. I like having the feeling that this young child needs me. I feel different today. It's a good different. I want to help Mona and I pray she can also help me.*

Mona glances at Dru who is busy preparing their pancakes. Dru looks happy today. Perhaps Dru is happy when she is busy and sad when she is not busy. Dru is a kind woman. She wants to make the world a better place. She has deep pain in her. Mona can sense this. Perhaps this pain motivates her to do good things for others. Mona is grateful that Dru took her in. *I hope she keeps me here. I don't want to find another home. I think that Dru and I can help one another. I pray that we can work together and live under one roof. I know Dru likes to read, and I am a reader. Maybe we can read together from time to time.* Mona lets out a sigh of relief and turns the next page in her book gently. A book is like a mountain, Mona thinks to herself, *I must conquer it.*

Mona puts her book down and joins Dru for breakfast. They face each other across the table.

"Thank you for making breakfast Dru. I am hungry and I like pancakes. My parents used to make pancakes."

"Tell me about your parents Mona. The only way I can understand who you are is by knowing who they are. Is it ok if we talk about them?"

"Of course! I love talking about them. My mom's name was Miranda, and my dad's name was Cole. My mom was short, about 5'3 and my dad was 5"10. My mom had brown hair like me, and my dad had green eyes like me. I look like both of them in some ways. They always showed me love. They talked about the land and the animals. They worked on a local ranch and were simple people. They loved to read, which is probably why I also love to read. They always taught me to be strong. I remember they said it is ok to cry, but then you have to get up and wipe away the tears. Mona remembers her parents telling her, life can be hard, but if you are strong, you will be ok. They would cook meals together; they would sing together. I have nothing but very positive memories of my mom and dad. I can say all of this with a huge smile because that is what they would want. What about your parents Dru?"

"Good question. My dad died when I was 7 years old. My mom remarried but my stepdad was mean. I felt like he did not want me, and I was a burden. I did not get a lot of love or attention. When I met Denny, he was my knight in shining armor. He was the best thing in my life. I placed him on a pedestal which is why I am grieving so hard. I never thought I would be without him."

Tears are streaming down Dru's face as Mona embraces her warmly.

"Thank you for sharing this with me Dru. I can help you be strong if you let me."

Dru nods her head, "I would like that, Mona. I need to learn how to do this. I will need time, but I see that you are strong. Please show me your ways."

Mona smiles and says "We can help one another. It will be like climbing a mountain. Sometimes, it will be very steep and other times we will find our way easily."

The Beat Goes On

Hope is in her hip-hop class. This is new to her. She always wanted to take hip-hop and never had the time. Hope looks around the class and sees mostly young people. She does not care anymore. She has officially reached that age where it does not matter. This class is on her bucket list.

The instructor is a middle-aged Hispanic man named Jessie. Jessie is fit and very upbeat. He is wearing a short-sleeved black shirt with grey sweats. His hair is a short crew cut. "You all ready for this class?" he bellows.

"I hope I can keep up with the class", says Hope and then laughs, "I didn't realize I said that out loud."

"No worries. Sometimes it's better to let me know what you really feel. My class incorporates all ages as you can see based on me. You should do fine."

Hope feels invigorated by the music. As the music ends, she wishes the class was still going. She realized during the class she no longer cared if she had the beat. She kept up to her own beat.

Jessie walks up to Hope. "How did you like the class?"

"I loved that class! I no longer cared if I was always keeping to the beat."

Jessie laughs, "That's the best way to do it. My wife was in the class. She was the tall blond in the front."

"She looks great for her age.

"She is twenty years younger than me."

"Are you kidding?"

"No, sometimes people are very perplexed and want to call her my daughter. The problem is that I am Hispanic, and she is white. This makes this situation all the more complex to them."

"Do you have any regrets?"

"No, I know who I am, and I know my culture. I have always liked younger, white women."

"Does she have any regrets?"

"I have noticed her looking at younger men lately and I feel she feels she might have missed out on something. The race card bothers her. I also worry about when I die, what will happen to her?"

"Does the race card bother you?"

"I wish the world did not look at people as colors, but unfortunately it does. I can brush it off. I have dealt with it for a long time."

"Why are you telling me this?"

"From one artist to another, put it in your book so that people think about this."

Hope grins, "What if there is no book? "

Jessie smiles, "What if there is not a hip-hop class next week?"

Hope nods, "I will see you at class. Thanks for sharing this with me. I will put it in my book. One more question, how did you know my book had anything about race in it? "

"As an artist, I see your soul; I can see that you are different and creative. I trusted my instincts and ran with it. Does this make sense to you?"

"As an artist, it makes all the sense in the world."

"How was the hip-hop class?" Brad asks as Hope enters their farmhouse.

"It was fun and invigorating. I will go again and again! I couldn't always keep up to the beat, but I did not care."

"Isn't that kind of like life?" Brad inquires.

"Yes, it really is. I also realize now that Calley is traveling my beat has become different."

"What do you mean?"

"My beat is slower. The days are going by so fast. I feel like I am making memories. I look at life so different. I miss Calley but have now adapted to where I am at this point in my life. I enjoy seeing family, friends, my book club, hiking and playing with our dogs. I have no time that I must be home. I have no time on the weekends that I must wake up. We have each other and I am so grateful for that. It doesn't mean that at some point, I do not want to move towards the mountains, but for now I am ok. Do you remember when Cal left? I never thought I would be, ok?"

"I remember that. I think it's a combination of things for you. The therapy has helped you. You also have to appreciate this time in your life and enjoy it. It's important to realize that life changes, the beat changes and to accept it. I am proud of you Hope for realizing that the beat goes on."

Sugar and Mountain come running up to Hope. They jump on her and lick her with kisses. Brad comes over and they kiss one another. Yes, the beat goes on thinks Hope for the first time since Calley left home.

The Day Thunder Came to Sundance

Sundance is curled up in a ball and Calley is holding her tight. Sundance is staring at Calley as Calley stares back at her. Calley notices that Sundance's eyes are watery and glazed. Sundance has been lethargic and not eating well. Calley has not taken her to see the vet yet. She is monitoring Sundance. It is the weekend, and she has not gone anywhere. She is very protective of her baby.

"I got you Sundance. I will always take care of you. I am sorry I had to leave you so many times, but now you can stay with me." Calley strokes Sundance's ears, and her belly. "I promise I will not leave you again."

Sundance continues to lay in Calley's arms. Calley continues to stroke her and talk to her. Calley notices when she leaves for work that Sundance panics. "I think she is afraid that I am going to leave her." Calley announces to Dakota.

Dakota comes over and strokes Sundance. He looks at the way she is curled up and at her eyes. "I think you are right Cal. The other thing I think that might help Sundance is another dog. What do you think? She needs a dog to play with and yet Sundance still has to feel like she is the queen, and she is your number one."

"I think you are right, but I know Sundance needs a little dog. She has always liked little dogs. It could be her baby and she would feel less intimated by a dog smaller than her. She could still feel like a queen. I am going to stay here all weekend with Sundance. You could go look at little dogs. I trust you."

"I'm glad you trust me Babe. It's taken us awhile to get to this level. I will go to the humane society and check out the dogs. I may bring a little dog home."

"I am excited to see how Sundance would react to a little dog. I think she would love it! "

"I thought you preferred bigger dogs."

"I do, but I have been watching Sundance and she prefers little dogs. This might do her some good and make her less anxious when I have to leave for work."

"Yeah, I think so too. I will call you from the humane society."

Dakota opens the door of the camper and gasps, "What the hell is this?" He is looking at a large burlap bag that is not fully zipped.

Calley and Sundance come to the door. Sundance jumps out of Calley's arms and barks. Sundance pushes on the camper door. "No Sundance, you stay here!" commands Calley as she exits the door.

Calley peers into the burlap bag and sees a little dog whimpering. "What kind of person would do this!" she exclaims.

Dakota reaches into the bag and gently pulls out the scared dog. She is dark brown with some black. Her eyes are dark She has small ears and a small tail. She curls up in his arms and cries more.

Sundance continues to bark. Calley turns to Sundance and says, "Stop barking so we can save this little dog!" Sundance lays down by the door and continues to watch.

"Calley, there are some items in the bag. See what they are."

Calley pulls out a piece of paper on which a note reads, *I live on the campground. I watch you both interact with Sundance every day. I do not know your names, but everyone on the campground knows your dog's name. She greets all of us. You were both born to raise dogs. Sundance needs a friend. This is Thunder, who is four-years old. I have had the privilege of raising her and can no longer continue, as I have a family emergency forcing me to return to my home state. I wanted to talk to you both one-on-one, but there was no time. I placed Thunder on your doorstep this morning. I know you rise early and will find her soon. She is up-to-date on all vaccines. I trust completely that Thunder will live a good life with you. I put her toys and dog food in this bag. I am not a coward. I am a dog lover who is now in a position that I never would have thought in my wildest dreams I would be in. I have a family member who died unexpectedly, and I now will be responsible for two small children. I never had kids, so I cannot try to raise kids and take care of my dog. Please take care of my baby as I know you will. I have also placed some money in an envelope in this bag for any additional food for Thunder. I wish I had the time to introduce myself to you, but Sundance knows me. Thank you for being dog lovers and for giving Thunder a home. Signed, a man of circumstances beyond his control who is trying to do the right thing.*

Calley and Dakota are sobbing as Calley finishes reading the note. They take Thunder into their camper.

Sundance senses the somber mood and kisses Calley and Dakota as they enter.

"What do you think Dakota of Thunder?"

"She is small and sweet. She is in good shape and her owner clearly loved the hell out of her."

"Yes, he did. There are so many people on this campground. I do not remember seeing Thunder before, but it does not matter. She is ours now. What a crazy situation, you were headed out to get a little dog and someone left one for Sundance!"

Dakota puts Thunder on the ground. Sundance comes over and sniffs Thunder. Sundance gives kisses to Thunder and seems to be familiar with her.

Calley scoops up Thunder and looks at her. "I never thought I would have a little dog, but my dog loves little dogs. Thunder, be good to Sundance and she will be good to you." Sundance barks and then jumps up and hugs Calley. "Oh, now you are feeling better. You just needed a little friend."

Calley pulls on her ponytail and grimaces, "Now we have two dogs! By the way, my Grandma Dru took in a thirteen-year-old girl to live with her. The girl's name is Mona, and she is from Montana. Her parents were killed in a car accident. She then went to live with her aunt in Iowa and this did not work out. Had my grandma not taken her in, she would have gone into foster care."

"Wow, that is a big deal. I think this is good for your Grandma Dru. She needs purpose all the time, as she defines herself by this. Mona will give her that purpose. Also, I did not have to go into foster care because my parents saved me. I wouldn't wish it on anyone. So how is your grandma doing with Mona?"

"I spoke with my grandma yesterday and she sounds less sad. She is busy with Mona. They seem to be good for one another. Mona will eventually go back to Montana when she is done with high school. She grew up on a ranch in Montana and loved it. Mona is exploring horseback riding in Iowa, as she doesn't want to lose her skills."

"Mona sounds like an interesting young girl. I never worked on a ranch, but I learned to ride horses with my dad. I love to ride horses and understand the skill that comes with riding. She should continue her lessons. We should take a trip to Iowa soon and see your family."

"I would love that! Right now, we have to see how Sundance and Thunder adjust to one another."

Dakota says, "Sundance definitely knows Thunder from the campground. She is not barking, and she is watching over Thunder. The man did the right thing by bringing Thunder to us. I will never understand the timing of this event, but maybe I am not supposed to.

Mona from Montana

Mona has become used to Dru's home. She knows every inch of it. Dru likes large aloe plants in brightly colored pots, and her home has many memories which live through the pictures on her walls. Dru has not made any changes to her home since Denny passed. Mona knows where Denny slept and where he spent most of his time in his home. He enjoyed his den where he read the latest politics news on the computer or watched TV. Mona knows what TV shows and movies he watched. Dru shared so many things about Denny with her.

The living situation has been good. Dru makes breakfast and dinner for her. Dru's cooking is wonderful, and Dru seems to be eating more now that Mona is there. Mona sees the deep sadness in Dru, but also the happiness when her son Brad stops by. Brad has a stepdaughter named Calley that Mona has not yet met. Calley travels for work as a park ranger. She has a dog named Sundance and a handsome boyfriend named Dakota. Dru said it took Calley forever to get a boyfriend as she was happy by herself. Calley loves the mountains, traveling and wildlife.

Mona is so impressed by Calley. She could listen to stories about her all day. Calley is the hero she never met. Mona is taken with Calley's beauty and her lifestyle. She heard Calley wishes to travel to Montana. This is a girl after her own heart. Dru talks about Calley often and Mona savors every story.

Mona also wants to start riding horses again. She was good at it and does not want to lose this skill. She has talked to Aunt Grace about the horseback riding. Aunt Grace and Mona have gotten along much better now that Mona is not under her roof. Aunt Grace has apologized for her breakdown and Mona has told her she understood that raising your brother's kid is not easy. Mona has told Grace that she likes living with Dru. Grace is happy to hear this. Grace has looked into horseback riding and has found a place where Mona can train. She will take her to this place on a weekly basis. Mona has thanked her and is excited. When she lived in Montana, she rode horses with her parents. It is a good memory and one that she cherishes. She pictures the three of them on their horses riding side by side with mom's hair blowing in the wind and dad with his cowboy hat. She remembers the trails they would take and each horse's personality. Mona's horse's name was Lightning, and she loved her horse. She has pictures of all the family horses and looks at them often. It helps Mona keep her cherished memories alive.

Dru knocks on the bedroom door and then enters.

"Are you looking at pictures Mona?"

"Yes, these are pictures of my parents on their horses. My horse's name was Lightning, and you can see her in the pictures too. My Aunt Grace is going to take me horseback riding on a weekly basis so that I can keep up on my riding skills. Would you like to see the pictures?

"I would love to see the pictures! I am so glad to hear about your Aunt Grace and your upcoming horseback riding lessons."

Dru looks through the pictures. This was one very happy family. They loved life on the ranch. Every picture shows their complete joy for their way of life. It almost makes you envious of their complete passion. Their love of the land on the ranch is evident. Dru is able to have a better understanding of Mona by looking at the pictures. As she finishes looking thought the pictures, she has tears in her eyes. "I am so glad you are going to ride horses again. I can see how important this is to you. What is it about the horseback riding that you loved?"

"I loved the freedom of riding. My hair blows in the wind, and I must control my horse, which helps me form a bond with the animal. It takes time and skill to master this. I must be able to trust my horse not to throw me off. Lightning was a light-brown color, and I would talk to her and groom her every day. I was very close to her."

Dru says to Mona, "I also groomed Denny. He had pain in his body, and he could no longer brush his hair, so I would brush it. This was one of my favorite things to do."

Mona and Dru hold each other's hands as they finish looking at Mona's pictures. Human touch is important. Dru took it for granted until Denny passed away. Dru now knows human touch is a gift.

Dru has been happier with Mona under her roof. It is nice to talk with her and have someone who understands grief. She is so impressed by how Mona handles her grief. She is a strong, young woman.

Dru continues to talk to her therapist who feels Mona is a good thing for Dru at this point in her life. The therapist likes how they talk about the loss of loved ones together and has encouraged Dru to also join a group of women her age to discuss the loss of a husband. The therapist realizes Dru may not do this and overall is glad that Dru has someone to talk to in Mona.

"Mona, do you want to go on a walk to the co-op? I am going to stop by my friend Cornelius's house to say hi. He is a man that I liked and wanted to date; I just couldn't do it. No one will ever be Denny. Cornelius now has a girlfriend named Sharon and they are doing well."

"Sure Dru, I will go with you." Mona pulls her brown hair into ponytail. She has on jeans, a sweatshirt and tennis shoes. She wears simple earrings that are small and delicate. She is not into makeup. "I am ready."

"That was quick, and you look good." says Dru.

"Thank you, Mona reacts with a smile. You look good too."

"I need someone to tell me that. Thank you, Mona. It's good to hear that. I am so glad you are living with me."

When they reach Cornelius's house, Sharon answers the door. "What are you doing here Dru? He is my man!"

"Sharon, I know this, and I am happy for you. I am just stopping by with my friend Mona who lives with me."

Sharon sees the young girl behind Dru.

"Oh! I apologize Dru. I don't usually act this way. I think as we get older, we change. I have become possessive. I am afraid to lose him. I don't want to be on my own again. We are doing well together. I did not mean to shout at you. He would be mad if he knew I acted like this towards you. This is what the loss of a loved one does. I lost my husband, and I am so grateful to have found Cornelius. I really needed him."

Sharon has tears streaming down her face and Dru does as well.

"Sharon, my husband is gone too, and I do not want anyone else. I have taken in Mona because she needed a home. We stopped by to say hello. I come as a friend."

"Hi Mona, I am so sorry you saw my awful behavior. I did not mean it."

"Hi Sharon, It's ok. I understand loss."

Cornelius comes to the door and smiles and then frowns. "Why is everyone crying?"

Sharon says, "I acted badly, and I was jealous of Dru and thought she was coming to take my man. I did not realize she had a child with her."

"Sharon, you got nothing to worry about. You're the best thing that has happened to me since Dorothy passed. I need you girl. Dru and I are friends. She knows she can stop by anytime. Who do you have with you Dru?"

"This is Mona. She is thirteen and lives with me now. It is working out well for both of us. She lost her parents in a car accident."

Cornelius exclaims with excitement, "Hi Mona! I know your parents were great people. Please cherish their memories each day. I think you and Dru will do well living together and helping each other. Would you like to come in and have some pancakes?'

"Sure, I love pancakes!" says Mona.

"Well then, you have come to the right place. I make some mean pancakes."

Soon they are eating at the wooden table and talking about Montana, horses, and all kinds of things.

Mona can see that Cornelius is a good person. She wishes Dru would have given him a chance, but she also sees how happy he is with Sharon. He reminds her of her parents. He is strong-willed and stubborn. He is a survivor and life must go on.

Dru and Mona leave hours later. Sharon again apologizes and Dru hugs her and tells her how happy she is for them both. Dru tells them to stop by her home anytime.

Mona looks at Dru as they walk toward the co-op. She seems fine. "Dru, are you ok after what happened with Sharon?"

"Yes Mona, I am good. Sharon did not mean it. I think they are good together. Cornelius is happy and found what he was looking for."

"Any regrets Dru? "

"Yes, I wish Denny was here and I had my guy."

"You know he cannot come back Dru, just like my parents cannot come back."

"In my head Mona, he is always with me."

"Dru you may be alone for the rest of your life if you think like this."

"Mona, I no longer care. He will always be in my head. I sleep with his pictures under my pillow."

Mona thinks about Dru and all that she has endured throughout her life. Dru had a rough childhood and Denny became her everything. Mona does not want a man to become her everything. Her parents were happy people who embraced life. If one of them had lived, he or she would have gone on. Not because they didn't love one another, but it is because when life gets tough, the tough get going.

Mona thinks about Cornelius and how happy he is. This is the person she wants to become. Mona thinks of a recent poem she read called the *Invitation by Oriah Mountain Dreamer*:

"It doesn't interest me what you do for a living. I want to know what you ache for and if you dare to dream of meeting your heart's longing.

It doesn't interest me how old you are. I want to know if you will risk looking like a fool for love, for your dream, for the adventure of being alive.

It doesn't interest me what planets are squaring your moon.

I want to know if you have touched the centre of your own sorrow, if you have been opened by life's betrayals or have become shriveled and closed from fear of further pain.

I want to know if you can sit with pain, mine or your own, without moving to hide it, or fade it, or fix it.

I want to know if you can be with joy, mine or your own; if you can dance with wildness and let the ecstasy fill you to the tips of your fingers and toes without cautioning us to be careful, be realistic, remember the limitations of being human.

It doesn't interest me if the story you are telling me is true

I want to know if you can disappoint another to be true to yourself. If you can bear the accusation of betrayal and not betray your own soul.

If you can be faithless and therefore trustworthy.

I want to know if you can see Beauty even when it is not pretty every day. And if you can source your own life from its presence.

I want to know if you can live with failure, yours, and mine, and still stand at the edge of the lake and shout to the silver of the full moon, 'Yes.'

It doesn't interest me to know where you live or how much money you have.

I want to know if you can get up after the night of grief and despair, weary and bruised to the bone and do what needs to be done to feed the children.

It doesn't interest me who you know or how you came to be here.

I want to know if you will stand in the centre of the fire with me and not shrink back.

It doesn't interest me where or what or with whom you have studied.

I want to know what sustains you from the inside when all else falls away.

I want to know if you can be alone with yourself and if you truly like the company you keep in the empty moments."

Mona dwells on this poem as she and Dru walk to the co-op. To be alive; that is really the gift that life gives you and what will you do with it? For now, Mona appreciates the roof over her head and has come to love Dru. Mona will never have her mom and dad again, but she has their memories, and she represents them.

"Mona, you seem like you are deep in thought. What are you thinking?" inquires Dru. Mona shares the poem she was thinking about with Dru.

"I love that poem and I Iove poetry. Would you like to listen to some live poets? I know a place by the campus where we could go?"

"I would like this Dru!"

"Poetry it is! We can go tonight." says Dru with a smile.

"Dru, can you tell me another story about your granddaughter Calley?"

"Yes, Mona. I am beginning to think that she is your hero."

Mona grins, "She is."

"Guess what Mona? I have better news than a story. Calley is coming to visit soon. She knows about you and wants to ride horses with you."

"What? When is she coming?"

"She will be here tomorrow, Mona."

"Dru, I am so excited! Has Calley ever ridden a horse before?"

"No, she says you will teach her."

Mona is now jumping up and down. "Sure, I will teach Calley! What if she rides better than me?"

"This is her first time on a horse."

"I know, I know! She seems to master everything."

Dru laughs and says, "I think you two will get along well."

Please Don't Wake Me Up from this Dream

Mona is staring at Calley. She takes in her style of dress, the national park t-shirt, the national park cap, the beautiful hair in a ponytail, the sweatpants and the Nike tennis shoes. Calley is tall and muscular. Her face is beautiful. Mona watches how Sundance follows Calley around the room. She also watches how the tall, handsome, dark man with the ponytail watches Calley. His name is Dakota. There is a little dog named Thunder that follows Sundance around.

They are at the farmhouse with Hope and Brad. The other dogs Sugar and Mountain are here. Mona has looked at many pictures of Calley but now seeing her in person is stunning. Calley is larger than life. Mona can see she loves both adventure and life. *Please, please* Mona thinks to herself, *don't wake me up from this dream. This is the best day of my life!*

Mona continues to watch Calley. She is talking to her mom and gives her a hug. Mona sees how happy Hope is to have her daughter home for a visit. Mona does not feel jealous that Calley's mom is alive, and her mom is not here. Mona knows how much her mom loved her. She observes Calley's strong, confident walk. *Oh!* She thinks to herself. *Calley is headed in my direction.*

"Hi Mona from Montana. I am Calley. How is your horseback riding going?"

Mona smiles with delight. "Hi Calley. I love horseback riding! The horse I used to have in Montana was named Lightning. The one I ride now is named Dust. When, I grow up I want to go back to Montana and work on a ranch."

"I was thinking about working on a ranch too. If I had not become a park ranger, I would have worked on a ranch. Good for you Mona. Can I watch you ride Dust?"

"Sure, you can watch me! Do you ride?"

"Not yet. I would like to learn, but the timing is not right at this point in my life. Is it difficult?"

"You have to get to know the horse and build trust."

"Yes, that is what I have heard. How long does it take?"

"It takes a lot of time and patience."

"That is what I thought. I will just watch you for now. I think it is cool that you ride horses. I am glad you are living with my grandma. She seems less sad and more like she has a purpose. Come meet my boyfriend and our dogs."

Mona is beaming from ear-to-ear. She is trying to hide her pride in walking with Calley, but it is impossible! And now she is going to meet Calley's boyfriend. She is not interested in boys, but Dakota is so handsome. She is almost drooling over him. She has to pull herself together before she meets him. Calley really is her hero!

Dakota is playing with the dogs. He is a natural with animals which Mona loves.

"Dakota this is Mona from Montana." says Calley.

"Hi Mona. It's good to meet you. I have heard a lot about you from Dru. It sounds like you look out for one another. That's good."

"Hi Dakota. Thank you." says Mona.

Calley looks at Mona and sees she thinks Dakota is hot. Mona is now fourteen. She probably has no interest in most men, but Dakota is not most men. Calley smiles at Dakota and winks. He winks back at her.

"So, Mona, I hear you ride horses?" inquires Dakota.

"I do. I love horses!" says Mona.

"I know how to ride also. It is a great skill. That is good that you are keeping up with it."

"Yes, I think so too. I just started riding again recently, but I feel comfortable with my horse, Dust," says Mona shyly. She doesn't want to look Dakota in the eyes. He is too handsome. She doesn't want Calley to know she thinks he is cute.

"Riding horses is the one skill Dakota has over me. His dad taught him when he was young," Calley explains.

Dru comes over and watches Mona interact with Calley and Dakota. She sees by Mona's facial expressions that she is awed by Calley. She also sees something she thought she would never see as Mona does not care much for boys. Mona thinks Dakota is hot. *Aw, to be fourteen again...* That was so many years ago for Dru. It is fun for her to watch Mona grow up.

Dru puts her arms around Calley and hugs her. Calley holds on to her grandmother. "Are you doing a little better with Mona around?"

"I am. I enjoy her company."

"Grandma, I am so happy to hear you say this! I did not think this day would come! Mona reminds me of myself in some ways."

"I agree Cal, she does. She loves a lot of the same things you do. She is a really cool kid."

"Yes, she is. How amazing it is the two of you found one another," says Calley.

"I think Denny must have sent Mona to look after me." Dru says.

"Maybe so grandma, maybe so," Calley replies.

Mona beams as she listens to the compliments about her coming from Calley. Mona gazes down the driveway and sees her Aunt Grace coming to join them.

She watches Grace walk up. Aunt Grace is so different from her dad. She is rigid, strict and set in her ways. Mona sighs and thinks of how Aunt Grace takes her to ride Dust. This has been a great bonding experience for the two of them. Aunt Grace doesn't ride, but she loves the beauty, strength, and freedom that the horse exhibit.

"Hi Aunt Grace. How are you?" Mona inquires as she embraces her with a hug.

Grace's brown hair is up in a bun. She is tall and lean. She has on jeans and a blue sweatshirt. Her feet are in comfortable brown loafers.

"I am good Mona. You look happy. I'm glad. Are you ready to go riding?"

"Yes, Dru and her family are going to come and watch me ride."

"Oh, that's good. You are an outstanding rider!" says Grace.

Grace introduces herself to everyone. The dogs all run up to her as well. She is a dog person, so she passes their test.

"Dru, Mona looks good. Thank you." says Grace.

"No, thank you. It's been good for me too." says Dru.

Dru and Grace hug tightly and without judgement. "Shall we watch Mona ride Dust?" Grace inquires.

"Yes, let's see Mona in action!" shouts Calley.

They are all at the pasture where Mona mounts Dust. Mona is a natural. She has a relationship with Dust which is evident. Her mounting style is graceful, and she rides with ease.

It is a beautiful late afternoon. The sky is clear, and everyone is absorbed in watching Mona ride Dust.

Mona has left this planet and is now only riding with Dust. This is how she feels when she rides. It is magical and now she has Calley watching her. It is a huge deal. Mona leans down and speaks to Dust, "Please don't wake me up from this dream." Dust snorts, which is her way of acknowledging whatever Mona wants. Mona beams and rides off into the clear blue skies.

The Fairgrounds

Ah, the Iowa fairgrounds. Food, people, rides, games, animals; so much to do and so much to see!

Hope and Brad are walking behind Dakota and Calley. Hope is taking in every detail of Calley and Dakota. She wants to remember everything so that when they leave to go back to work, she has their memories. She watches her daughter's gait, the way Calley looks at Dakota and the way he looks at her. The words between them are unspoken, but yet spoken through a look or a simple glance at one another.

Hope notices another dynamic as she always has because she is the mother of a lovely biracial child, and she must take this into account. The crowd at the fair is predominantly white. Sure, there are other people of other races, but not many. Hope again questions herself as to whether she did the right thing by moving back here when Calley was young.

Brad has never cared about the people watching at the fairgrounds. He is more interested in what food is available. Hope and Brad stop at various food stands to see what is available. The fresh corn is always good! Brad thinks about his mom and Mona. Their relationship seems to be working and he is relieved. He is also glad to have Calley home for a visit. He knows it means the world to Hope.

Calley is happy to be at the fairgrounds as she has not been here in years. She notices the stares from time-to-time from white folks who may or may not be judging her. She has experienced this for years. She no longer lives here so it is different. She can choose to leave it. She looks at Dakota and realizes that he too notices the stares on occasion. He brushes it off and moves on.

Dakota notices Calley people watching. He does it as well. The fairgrounds are a good place to do this. So much is going on at the fairgrounds... kids running around, food, animals, and rides. He would rather be on a hiking trail where it is peaceful.

Dru and Mona walk behind Hope and Brad. Dru reminisces on her time with Denny at the fairgrounds. She remembers how they held hands, what they ate, what rides they went on, and what animal events they watched. Dru shares this with Mona who listens to all of her stories.

The fairgrounds do not remind Mona of anything. Her parents did not go to the fairgrounds. They were too busy on the ranch. She likes to people watch at the fairgrounds. She watches the different people and imagines what their lives are like. Dru continues to talk about Denny and Mona listens. She is used to this talk by now and it does not bother her. Dru needs to do this, and Mona appreciates Dru and feels that she is doing her a favor by listening just as Dru did her a favor by taking her in.

Mona likes to look at the people as they walk by and imagine what kind of lives they live. *Are they happy? Are they putting on an act? Did any of them lose their parents? Do they ride horses?* As a horse lover, she feels she can pick out the folks that ride. She then looks ahead to watch Calley again. She and Calley have formed a bond in the short time that Calley has been visiting. Mona turns to Dru, "Dru I am going to walk with Calley for a while. I am going to miss her when she leaves. I want to get some more time with her."

Dru smiles, "Of course Mona, of course."

Dru watches Mona run up by her granddaughter. She sees Calley grin at her, and they walk together. Mona is different with Calley. Mona is sure of herself and projects a stronger woman when she is with Calley.

Dru looks into the oncoming crowd and sees Cornelius, Sharon, Jaxton, Jade, and Jade's kids smiling and coming toward her. Dru beams and stops to give hugs and say hi. The others see Cornelius and also come over to say hello.

Brad again wishes his mom would have chosen to stay with this man. Although, Dru does not seem to care about Sharon, she seems to like the friendship she shares with the family.

Calley sees the contentment in Cornelius's face and observes how his family seems relaxed. Perhaps he did the right thing by going with Sharon. It is another color thing? Her grandma seems better now that Mona is around.

Calley and family continue walking the fairgrounds. Calley thought the occasional stares at her and Dakota from some of the white people were over with until she saw a Hispanic man with a white woman. The woman was younger and very attractive. The woman couldn't be his daughter, so they had to be an item. There were a lot of white guys looking at this couple and they seemed to have an issue with this girl being with this man.

"Damn, his life must be difficult," Calley comments to Dakota. Mona was still walking with Calley, so she was careful to say this softly to Dakota.

"His life is only difficult if he wants it to be. He gets to make that choice," remarks Dakota.

Calley watches her mom run up to this man with the hot white girl and give him a hug. "Hi Jessie. This is my family." Hope introduces each person.

Hope looks at Calley and says, "Jessie is my hip-hop teacher, and this is his wife, Mercy."

Of course, his wife's name is Mercy. She is going to need mercy to get through the choice they made of getting together and the way some people look at them. Calley thinks to herself.

Her out loud voice says "Hi Jessie and Mercy. Nice to meet you. Jessie, how did you get into teaching hip-hop?"

"That is an easy question. I love the way music takes you away from the normal. When you dance you can be anywhere you want to be. It is the music that moves me. "

Calley smiles and nods her head. She now understands how Jessie and Mercy make their life work. They are dancing their way through this crowd.

Never Thought This Would Happen

Calley, Dakota, Sundance and Thunder are back on the road. They are leaving Iowa and heading to Florida

This is their last trip before they have to return to work. This is a trip neither of them could have predicted and yet it came together easily. They are going to meet Calley's dad. Dakota's parents are going to meet them in Florida as well. Dakota's parents love to travel and will be in Florida at the same time as Calley and Dakota.

"I'm nervous to meet your parents, Dakota."

"You shouldn't be Calley, they are great people."

"Are you nervous to meet my dad? "

"No, I am sure your dad is easy to get along with."

"Yes, he is. He will like you."

"Just as my parents will like you Cal."

Sundance and Thunder bark in unison.

"Yes girls, everyone is going to be excited to see you!" says Calley.

"Did you have a good time in Iowa, Dakota? "

"Of course, babe, I love your mom, stepdad, grandma, Mona, Cornelius, and family. I am not much for the fairgrounds though."

"What is it that you don't like about the fairgrounds? I feel like I am being judged. I would rather be out hiking. I like animal watching, not people watching."

"Me too babe, me too."

Dakota puts on reggae music and drives for ten hours. They pull over at a rest stop and sleep. Next, Calley puts on rap music, and she drives ten more hours. Both dogs are good travelers. They stop from on occasion to get food and walk their dogs.

"Dang Dakota; between the both of us, we made good time driving."

"We really did Cal. It's amazing what we can do together."

"I never thought this would happen."

"What do you mean?"

"I never thought I would meet someone that I feel so complete with, has met my mom and stepdad, and soon, my dad!"

"Calley, I could only have dreamed of someone like you. Girl, you are perfect for me."

Calley smiles and says, "This is my dad's house coming up on the right." Dakota looks and takes in his surroundings. The neighborhood is full of black and brown folks. The house is modest, and he sees a man outside working on a car. The man has a stocky build, is tall and has a full head of thick, black hair. His skin is dark brown. The man keeps working on the car as Calley pulls up.

Calley parks and everyone exits the truck.

"I am going to sneak up on him. He works hard and tunes out everything." Calley whispers to Dakota.

Calley goes behind her dad and taps him on the shoulder. He turns around and smiles wide. He wipes his hands on his overalls and takes off the grease.

"Calley, you're here and you brought a friend!"

Calley and her dad embrace.

"Dad, this is Dakota, and you already know Sundance. This is our new little dog, Thunder."

"I didn't know you liked little dogs."

"I don't Dad, but Sundance does."

"I see that. So, you picked a good partner for Sundance. Hi Dakota, welcome to my home. Come on in. My mom made sago porridge."

"Hi, Andres. It is good to meet you. Calley has told me a lot about you."

"All good, I'm sure." says Andres.

"Yes sir." Dakota nods as he and Calley enter the house.

Dakota notices that Andres still has an accent. He realizes as he enters his home and looks around that his native country is important to him. There are many symbolic items of Guyana. He notices the Guyanese flag displayed on the wall, the hot sauce on the kitchen table, and a small area rug with the flag of Guyana which is displayed in the living room.

Calley explains to Dakota that sago porridge is a warm food made by simmering milk, spices, and sago pearls until thickened. Sugar is added to thicken it.

Calley also explains even though she is vegan, she never says anything about the milk. This is the way her Grandma Iona cooks, and she shuts her mouth.

Grandma Iona enters the room. She has a very pretty face, dark skin, and thick gray hair. Her eyes sparkle when she hugs Calley, and her face lights up as she meets Dakota.

"Come eat Calley and Dakota." Grandma Iona says.

Dakota hears her heavy accent as well. Calley really does live in two different worlds: one in Iowa and one in Florida. Both are good and yet so different. Perhaps this is what makes Calley the person she is, a spiderweb of complexity, beauty, and intelligence. He watches how Andres interacts with his mom. He takes care of her, and she lives in his home. Calley has talked to Dakota about Grandma Iona and has said she is not sure where she stands on how her dad cares for his mother. She sees the good part of it where her dad looks out for his mom; however, his living situation has also cost her dad relationships and Calley is afraid he may live alone after his mom passes. Calley discussed with Dakota how difficult it was for her mom to live with her Grandma Iona many years ago, although Hope still loves and respects her.

Andres has dated other women, but none have stayed with him and many times it has been because of his living situation.

However, Andres has never complained to Calley about not having a woman in his life. He has told her he is ok by himself. Andres has had to take his mom to the hospital on many occasions. Calley worries about all the stress her dad has taken on with his mom. She feels he would be less stressed if Grandma Iona were in a nursing home.

Calley's dad runs an automotive business out of his home. He has several loyal customers who have used his automotive repair services for years. He loves his work and Calley has helped him repair cars many times. Once, she was able to diagnose the car's problem before he did. She will never forget this moment. She was very proud, and her dad was also.

"So how long have you been dating my daughter?" Andres asked Dakota.

"Long enough to know she is stubborn, driven, beautiful and so damn smart," answers Dakota.

Grandma Iona and Andres laugh and nod their heads.

"Did you meet on the job?" Andres inquires.

"Yes, Dad, we did. I didn't want anyone in my life. I was doing fine, but Dakota kept pushing and I have to admit, my life is so much better with him," Calley responds.

"You're glowing, Baby, and I am happy for you." says Andres.

"Thank you," says Calley and Dakota with grins on their faces.

"Dakota's parents are vacationing in Florida. They are an hour away so I will be meeting them for the first time tomorrow."

"Are you nervous, Calley?" Andres questions.

"No, Dad, I just never thought this would happen."

"Life is like this, Calley. You cannot predict it. Most of the time things happen when you least expect it. You will both have to make a trip with me at some point to Guyana."

"We want to do that, Dad. Dakota has been there before and liked it."

"Ah, that's good to hear. We will go together when the timing is right for me. I have to wait until my business slows down. I am busy right now."

"That sounds good, Dad. You can let us know when you are ready. What will you do about Grandma Iona when you go to Guyana?"

"I will have my cousin look after her while I am gone."

"It will be nice for you to get way. Do you want to come with us tomorrow and meet Dakota's parents?"

"I'm afraid to leave my mom by herself. I better stay here so that I can work and be around if she needs something. Are you coming back to me after your visit with Dakota's parents?"

"Yes dad, we may be with them for two days, but then we will come back and spend more time with you and Grandma Iona."

"That's good, Baby. I always like it when you are here."

"I have good news for both of you," says Dakota. "My parents can come to us. There is an RV camp nearby where they will stay. Then we do not have to travel an hour to see them. They would like to meet everyone."

Calley smiles and looks at Dakota, "That just made this trip a whole lot easier."

Andres looks at this daughter and sees that she loves this man whether she has told him, or he has told her, they love one another. He is happy for her. He has always wanted Calley to have someone by her side. Andres did not know if it would happen because she is strong-willed and mechanical.

"What tribe are you and your parents from, Dakota?" asks Andres.

Calley jumps in and says, "If it's ok, I am going to answer this Dad."

"Hold on Calley, it is his parents. Let the man answer."

Dakota grins, "My parents are both white and they adopted me a long time ago. I decided not to search for my birth parents, and I have accepted my foster parents as my own. They love me and they have always been there for me. Both my parents are history professors and we have researched a lot about my people who are from the Navajo tribe. I love my people and my parents."

"That is interesting, Dakota. I look forward to meeting them. They did a good job raising you," says Andres.

"Thank you, Andres. I appreciate that coming from you. My parents' names are Barb and Don. That is their RV pulling up to your house. They are here!"

"Oh, what! I didn't think they were coming yet," remarks Calley. "I am so damn nervous. You should have given me more time, Dakota!"

"I didn't know they were coming this quick, Cal or I would have. They like to surprise me sometimes."

"Come on Calley, let's head outside and meet them, "says Andres.

"Ok, Dad. I am coming," says Calley with a stone face.

"Cal, I have been meaning to ask you something." says Dakota quietly so that Andres cannot hear.

"What is it, Dakota?"

"Why do you treat your dad with more respect than your mom?"

"Oh, dang, I did not see this question coming. You know I love my mom."

"Yes, I know this, but I see a difference in the treatment. Your dad gets a lot of respect, and you are running around later to bring him some Ital Jamaican food."

"My dad gets this respect because he is brown. My mom is white. My dad has more struggles to face because of his color. This is how I look at it. Does this make me a bad person?"

"No, I feel you and I'm glad you answered. Now let's go meet my white-ass parents to whom I have always shown respect, but then, I never knew my real parents."

Barb is tall with brown hair pulled back in a ponytail. She has a pretty face. She has a button nose. Her eyes are dark brown with long lashes. Her mouth is thin but when she smiles, she lights up the room. Don is tall; he has bright blue intelligent eyes that seem to look into your soul. He has a broad roman nose, as if carved into his face. His hair is strawberry red, and he wears it in a buzz cut. Both parents have some streaks of gray hair, but they look good for their ages which would be in their late fifties. Barb and Don embrace their son. He smiles and hugs them back.

Calley and Andres introduce themselves and Don and Barb are delighted to meet them. Andres asks everyone to come to his backyard where he has chairs and there is shade from the summer heat. Andres gets everyone a drink. He has iced tea which is welcomed by all.

Calley is surprised by how easy it is to talk with Dakota's parents. They are travelers and she finds she is enjoying her conversation with them. She also notices his parents could care less about the black and brown people in the neighborhood. Their son is brown, and they love him and accept everything because of their love for him. This is like my mom and my stepdad, thinks Calley. They could care less because they love me, and I am brown. Calley watches her dad interact with Dakota's parents. He does so easily. Andres's friends are white, brown, and black. He has never had trouble with race. It's strange because Grandma Iona is always talking about race. She prefers the people of her country. She is distrustful of other people. Calley has never heard her dad talk like this.

"I am going to get my dad Jamaican Ital food. Can I get you some food as well?" Calley inquires of Dakota's parents.

"Yes, of course we like Ital food. Do you want us to come with you?" Barb asks.

"No, there is a place right around the corner and I will bring it back and we can eat outside," says Calley.

"I am going to go help Calley get the food," says Dakota.

"Ok son, see you when you get back," says Don.

"I never thought Dakota would find someone. I am grateful that he found your daughter. She is beautiful, strong, intelligent and they have similar passions," says Barb.

"Yes, Calley is all of that. She can also work on cars with ease. I am a master mechanic and I love cars. She's got her love of cars from me. Some people struggle with a girl who can fix a car, but your son seems ok with it."

Barb and Don laugh, "He is more than ok with it. He is head over heels in love with her."

Andres chuckles, "Yes, I noticed the love they have for one another too. They are a lucky couple, and they look good together."

"Yes, they do!" says Barb.

"So, your mom lives with you, Andres?" Don questions.

"Yes, I would have you meet her, but I think she is laying down. She has been living with me for a long time. My parents divorced a long time ago."

"That was good of you to take her in," comments Don.

"Well, my mom can't hear me out here, so I will be honest with you. I did it for all the right reasons, but it has caused me a lot of relationships and is a lot of work. One of the main reasons Calley's mom left was because she did not want to keep living with my mom. She loved my mom, but she wanted her own space. Other women have also left for the same reason. Anytime my mom is sick, I have to rush her to the doctor or hospital. I work out of my home, so I am lucky. My whole life revolves around her."

Don says, "Andres, I can relate to this in a different way. My mom lives on her own and I worry about her. We live in the same state, and I thought about moving her in with Barb and I, but knew our lives would no longer be our own. Initially, I felt selfish, but I have made peace with it. We go to see her as much as possible."

Andres nods in agreement.

Calley and Dakota arrive with the Ital food, which is the vegan Rasta Pasta, one of Andre's favorites. They all sit down outside at the table to enjoy the food. There is a beautiful sunset as their backdrop.

Dreams That I Wish Were Real

I could stare at the complexity of a spider web for hours. Every intricate web so delicate and yet so strong. I try to claw through the webs, but I am now covered in them. I run and now find myself in the northern trees, tall trees that I have to fight my way through. The branches ripping into my skin as I run and climb my way out. I look up. These are some of my favorite trees, oak, hickory, ironwood, and maple. Their strong branches and heavy roots are something I marvel at. I have made it through the trees! I can now see the mountains which are so magnificent that I weep. I see homes by the mountains, and I look for Calley and Dakota. No, my daughter does not want to be locked into a home. I see RVs and I head down this path. "Calley, Calley!"

Hope wakes up in bed and calls for Calley. Brad responds, "Hope, you are dreaming again! Calley is not here. She is in Florida with her dad and Dakota's parents."

"Yes, I know that. Sometimes I have these vivid dreams that seem so real. I see tangled spider webs and tall northern trees that then turn into mountains which I have to cross in my dreams. In my dream last night, Calley was here. I think because I dream so vividly, sometimes, I believe my dreams are true. I was asking Calley and Dakota about going on a hike. We lived in the mountains. All the dogs were there. We were happy and life was good."

"Here is the good part, Hope, we are happy, and I know you miss your daughter. There may be a time when we move, but we cannot do it yet. The other problem you have is that Calley and Dakota may stay in one state for a while, but then, due to their jobs, can be called to another national park."

"I know Brad. I just wish I could spin a web where we could all be in one place. That is probably why I do it in my dreams. Overall, my menopause is better. I can now sleep at night. I have a great therapist. I love my hip-hop class, my gardens, my friends, my family, our dogs, and you."

"I spoke to Calley last night and she was with Dakota's parents, her dad, and she seems happy." says Brad.

Hope says, "I wonder why she didn't call me last night."

"She did call you, but you were outside playing with the dogs, and I talked to her for a while."

"That is good to hear. I am glad you spoke with her. I struggle with middle age. It's hard to adjust. You get so used to your old life and it's hard to realize you can have a new one. Then you also start thinking about the people around you who are getting sick and dying. You realize how limited our time is on this planet. Look at how much your mom changed once she lost Denny!"

"I know, Hope, but at least now she has Mona. Who would have thought this would have happened and that it is working. Now, I worry about what happens when Mona eventually goes back to Montana, but you cannot live like this," says Brad.

"You're right Brad. That's a good point about your mom. It is working well for now and Mona should be here for about four years. We must not dwell on the future but accept the present."

The phone rings and Hope grabs it. It is Calley.

"Hi honey."

"Hi Mom." I can tell from her voice that something is wrong, and I know it is early in the morning for her to call. "What is it?"

"My dad is in the hospital."

"Oh Calley, what happened?"

"He was sleeping, and I went in to check on him. He was not breathing. I performed CPR but it didn't work. I am at the hospital now with him. Dakota is here. Dakota's parents are at the campground. Grandma Iona is a mess. I think my dad is too stressed out taking care of her."

"Calley, is he breathing now?"

"I am waiting for the doctors to come out." I can hear the tears pouring down her face. "Here comes a doctor now. Hold on."

I wait and I pray for a miracle.

Dakota comes on the phone, "Hope, Andres is gone."

"Dakota! What happened?"

"He passed away as he had difficulty breathing. They will know more when the doctors return."

"And Calley?" says Hope.

"She is curled in a ball on my lap and cannot talk to anyone right now."

"We will be on the next plane."

"No, Calley wants time to process this. We will call you."

Brad is near me and has heard everything. In a minute, the life we knew is gone. Calley is not here. I cannot hold her, comfort her. My heart breaks for Andres. My heart breaks more for my daughter. She is too young to have lost her father. What will Andres's mom do now? My head is spinning. I grab the edge of my bed and cry. I want to go back to my dreams where things were happier. I was able to get through the spider webs and the trees. I saw the mountains. Where I lay crying now, there is no beauty, only stinging pain!

Numbness Through and Through

Calley is numb as she lays on Dakota's lap. She thinks of Grandma Iona who she now knows has died of a broken heart after hearing that Andres died. Calley is still at the hospital. She was with her dad as the team tried to revive him. She thinks of the hospital team that tried to save him. She pictures his face over and over again. She replays every last minute of his life until her head hurts. She cried in the room. Now she is spent and drained. The death of her Grandma Iona hurts but is not surprising and is probably the best outcome for her grandma. Now she is sorry for herself. She has to go on without her papa. There will be no upcoming trip to Guyana with him, no more running to get him Ital food, no working on cars with him, and no phone calls to or from him. Sure, she will see his cousins and family members in Guyana and in Florida, but her dad and her brown identity are forever gone!

She is young. She planned to have him in her life for a long time. Should she have spent more time with him? What could she have done to save him? A thousand questions fill her head.

She will never get to look at her dad again, to see his eyes light up as she tells him about her job or what is wrong with a car. They had a beautiful time with Dakota's parents who are still alive! Her dad liked Dakota and was happy for her. He only met Dakota once! Why is Dakota's dad still alive and her dad gone! What kind of world is this?

Dakota looks down at Calley and holds her fiercely. He is deeply worried about her. "Calley, you need to shout from the mountain tops that this is unfair and that you love your dad forever. Don't keep this inside, don't let it tear you apart. I am here for you."

Hope shouts, "Calley! I'm here, Baby."

Dakota and Calley look up to see Hope running towards them. Hope puts her arms around her daughter as Calley lays in Dakota's lap.

"Dakota, thank you for taking such good care of my daughter."

"I always will Hope."

Hope nods and says, "Somehow I knew you would say that."

"Mom are you here by yourself?".

"Yes Baby, I had to be here for you."

Calley tearfully exclaims, "I told you to wait."

"I could not wait because I needed to know that you were ok."

"Mom, I miss Dad so much." Calley's tears flow freely.

"This is why I am here Cal. I know how much you loved your dad. You are too young for this. You did not deserve this. I also know how much he loved you and how proud he was of you. What can I do for you?"

"Nothing Mom, I think I am in shock."

"I am not going anywhere."

Dakota strokes Calley's hair as she continues to cry silent tears. Hope cries voiceless tears as well. Dakota wipes away the tears that are forming in his eyes as he tries to be strong.

"Mama, I miss my damn dog!" Calley suddenly announces.

Dakota and Hope look at one another and Dakota says, "Calley, we can leave the hospital and go to the RV park where my parents are. Sundance is there."

"Yes, I am ready to go see my dog."

Dakota and Hope help Calley to her feet. They walk out of the hospital. As they reach the RV park, Sundance comes running up to Calley. Sundance jumps up on Calley and gives her hugs and kisses. Calley scoops Sundance into her arms and holds her. Calley cries into her fur.

Barb and Don come running. They observe the scene and say nothing aloud.

Barb whispers to Dakota. "Sundance sniffed the air and must have known Calley was coming, she jumped out of the RV and ran in Calley's direction. We could not stop her."

Dakota says, "It's ok Mom, it's what Calley needed."

Hope stands next to Calley and Sundance and observes the deep love. Calley looks up at her mom, "Remember I rescued Sundance in Florida while I was visiting my dad. Truthfully, I think Sundance may have rescued me in so many ways."

"The bond that you share is incredible, Calley, just like the bond that you shared with your dad."

"I feel like I lost the brown part of me."

"You still have all your dad's relatives in Florida and Guyana. You still have me. I know I am not brown, but I raised you and therefore I became brown on the inside. You cannot raise a child of color without becoming a piece of them. Your love for your child defies everything. You should always make time to see your dad's relatives and keep in contact. I have many precious memories of Grandma Iona which I will share with you."

"Grandma Iona needed my dad to survive, and she could not live without him. When he died, her heart broke and that was it. I was not surprised, but rather relieved that she did not suffer long."

"I felt the same way Cal. Will you keep your dad's ashes?"

"Yes, I will keep them with me at all times. Mom, when I look at you, your eyes are different. You now have a deep sadness in them."

"That's a good observation. When someone you care deeply about passes, a piece of your soul does too. I see the look in your eyes. I saw it in Grandma Dru's eyes when she lost Grandpa Denny. As I was checking in at the airport, someone in the ticket line said I am sorry for your loss. I asked how do you know? She said responded she lost someone also and she can always see this loss in someone's eyes."

"Do you know where my dad's ashes will go, Mom?"

"I have a guess. You will put them in a collar around Sundance's neck."

"How did you know?"

"You treasured your dad, and you treasure Sundance, so it makes sense."

"My Uncle Santino will move into my dad's home. He will keep it the same way to preserve memories."

"That is so important, Calley. Make sure you visit the home as often as you can. What did Uncle Santino say about the funeral?"

"It will take place in Guyana, and it will be a celebration of life where there is a period of nine nights when friends and family come to the home of the deceased. In this case, it will be the family home in Guyana. Are you coming?"

"Yes, Calley. Brad and I will both be there to honor your dad's life. I like the fact that in Guyana, it is nine nights. It gives us more time to celebrate your dad."

Calley says, "I am glad you came, even though I told you not to. I needed you."

Calley and Hope embrace with Sundance in the middle as Sundance refuses to leave Calley's arms.

The Coda Symbol

Barb, Don, Hope, Calley and Dakota go to Andres's favorite local jazz club. It brings familiarity to Calley, and the music soothes her broken soul. She reminisces about times she spent here with her dad. Everyone listens as Calley speaks, as they know she needs to share all of her memories with them. This is how she keeps Andres alive. This is how she stays alive.

Hope looks around the club and notices the coda symbol. A coda is an oval-shaped musical symbol with oversized crosshairs and is used to organize complex musical repetitions. In music, coda is a passage that brings a musical composition to an end. This symbol is another sign that represents the end of Andre's life in Hope's mind.

Calley's hair is down, her eyes are sad, and she has on a light blue sweatshirt and a pair of jeans. Her head rests on Dakota's shoulder. Hope sits next to her and rubs her back.

Uncle Santino walks into the club and joins the table. He holds Calley in his strong arms for a long time and tells her how much he loves her. He says hi to Hope and meets Dakota and his parents. "Calley, I miss Andres. I miss talking to him about cars, I miss drinking with him, I miss his larger-than-life presence. You know your dad would fill the room when he entered. When I am in his house, I feel his presence everywhere. I also miss Grandma Iona. She was a good soul. Calley, you were your dad's pride and joy. He went too soon! Cherish every memory and keep him alive by talking about him. Celebrate his life."

The entire table has tears welled up in their eyes. Hope thinks of Andres and struggles to believe that he is gone. She fights to know how best to support her daughter. No one prepares you for death.

"Calley, do you know you can have the house and live in it?" says Uncle Santino.

"I know, but Dakota and I love our jobs. We also love to travel. I am a child of two worlds. One is my mom's world, and one is my dad's world. When I am in nature, I am a child of one world. The mountains call me, and I run towards them. I find all my strength and stability in the national parks. I sleep in a camper at night. I look up at the stars. I am not ready to put a permanent roof over my head yet. I know the house is for me and when I am ready, I will settle down. I will continue to see you and all of Daddy's relatives. The Monte Carlo can stay in the garage for me. I have nowhere to put it right now. My dad and I worked on that car so many times together. I love that car."

"I remember Andres talking about the Monte Carlo. He could talk about your car expertise forever! I would like all of you to come over tonight and have dinner with me. You could also stay in Andre's house until we leave for Guyana."

Nine Nights

Calley loves Guyana and has been here many times. This time it is without her dad. It feels raw and unsettling. She is grateful that Dakota, her mom, stepdad, Dru, Mona, and Uncle Santino have accompanied her on this trip. She has never felt so vulnerable in her young life. She always thought she was so strong, but the death of her dad has crippled her emotions and her strength. She knows that Sundance and Thunder will be taken care of well by Barb and Don who remained in Florida to care for them.

The Nine Nights in Guyana is rich in tradition. Nine Nights is also known as Dead Yard. It is an extended wake that lasts for several days with roots in African religious tradition. During this time, friends and family come to the childhood home of Andres. There are pictures of Grandma Iona and Andres in the front of the home with candles lit in remembrance of their lives. Friends and family members from Andres's native country share their condolences and memories while singing hymns and eating food together.

Grandma Dru admires this rich tradition and wishes that Denny could have had something like this versus the traditional funeral. They have reached the end of the Nine Nights and Calley has cried until she cannot cry anymore.

Hope is now watching Calley with somber eyes and tears that can no longer come to the surviving parent who must put on her shield of armor and be strong for her daughter.

Mona walks over to Calley and taps her gently on the shoulder. "Calley, you are the strongest girl I know. You are my hero."

"Mona, I am broken, but I will survive. You lost both of your parents and you are so strong. I am glad you came to Guyana. It means a lot to me."

Dakota, Brad, and Grandma Dru walk over to Calley. They hold her and say nothing. There are no words, and she knows they love her.

"Mom, how do you feel?" inquires Calley as she wanders over to her mom.

"I can get up each day and do what I need to do. Sometimes, I feel like I am just going through the motions. Death is unfathomable, intangible, and raw. I hurt that your dad is not here anymore. I feel like you were robbed. How do you feel?"

"There are days where I feel I am going through the motions, but then I have other days where I wake up next to a beautiful man, stand beside a strong family, kiss my favorite dog in the world, plan my next hiking trip, eat my favorite food, and work on my next car. These parts of me want to live."

"Baby, that is the most amazing thing I have heard you say. You will survive this with your passions. How did you feel about the Nine Nights, Calley?"

"I loved it. It gave me a lot of time to hear stories about my dad, talk about him and celebrate him. I loved the stories that Uncle Santino shared about them growing up in Guyana. I prefer it over the funeral customs in the United States."

"I also enjoyed it. I had more time to process the grief and the stories helped me remember Andres."

Grandma Dru approaches and hugs Calley. "Cal, I loved Nine Nights. You honor the dead better in Guyana then we do in the United States."

Calley says to everyone, "I want to take you to the waterfall that my dad loved to spend time at when he visited Guyana, which is a short walk from the house."

Everyone proceeds towards the waterfall and takes in the natural beauty. The water symbolizes so much to each of them. Calley feels her dad's presence. Dru wishes Denny was here to help her get through this. She thinks he may be watching her from the waterfall. Mona feels a strong bond with nature and with Calley. Dakota runs up behind Calley and takes her hand. He says nothing. Brad joins Hope and they watch the others. "How are you doing, Hope?"

"I am angry! I am so pissed that Calley lost her dad. I can't be a mom and a dad. I feel like I have to lose weight, take good care of myself so I can be here for my daughter. I need to eat better. I need to listen to her feelings more. Why is Andres gone? You look at all the people we know that drink, smoke, or have major health issues and they are still here. It does not seem fair. I want to wave a magic wand and bring Andres back! I can't find the wand and I cannot find the magic. At the same time Brad, I want to thank you for being an amazing stepdad, for helping me to raise Calley, for always being a presence in her life."

"You're welcome and I feel the same way you do about Andres. I can't comprehend it. I want to make sense of it, and I cannot."

"There is no fixing this, Brad. We must go onto the next chapter. We must always keep Andre's memory alive."

<h1 align="center">The Next Chapter</h1>

Dakota, Calley, Mona, Dru, Brad, Hope, Barb, Don, Thunder, and Sundance are seated at the campground in Florida. It is a cool evening, and they have a fire going.

"Pain is inevitable. Suffering is Optional."
- Buddha

"Death is not the end.
Death can never be the end.
Death is the road.
Life is the traveler.
The Soul is the Guide."
-Sri Chinmoy

Hope is pondering the two Buddhist poems that Barb and Don are sharing with her. She recently began digging deeper into the Buddhist teachings, such as pain and gain, love and loss. These sayings make sense to her and help her deal with death. Barb and Don are not practicing Buddhists, but they also believe in many of the teachings.

Calley is speaking about Uncle Santino. She shares that she feels good about him taking care of her dad's house. When she walks through her dad's house, she has so many memories of him, and she senses his presence. She can smell him. She can see him. She will go back to his house soon to visit and spend time with her uncle. She would like to paint the Monte Carlo blue, and yes, Dakota can come with her when she goes. If she gets married to Dakota and they have a boy, they will name him Andres in memory of her father. This is a long time away and she is not yet ready, but for the first time in her life it is a concrete thought. Sundance is on her lap and the collar around Sundance's neck holds Andre's ashes. It is a simple collar, one that you would not expect to hold ashes, but it suffices. Calley lovingly pets Sundance and stares down at the collar with warm memories and love. Calley looks around the campfire and knows without the love and support of everyone here, she would not be well. She needs their support, love, and the guidance. She now realizes for the first time that life is incredibly complex and fragile. She loves nature and is ok by herself, but there will be many times when she needs the people of her two worlds to be by her side.

Barb and Don read a poem to the group as the fire flickers in and out:

"May death come gently towards you,
Leaving you time to make your way
Through the cold embrace of fear
To the place of inner tranquility.
May death arrive only after a long life
To find you at home among your own
With every comfort and care you require.
May your leave-taking be gracious,
Enabling you to hold dignity
Through awkwardness and illness.
May you see the reflection
Of your life's kindness and beauty
In all the tears that fall for you.
As your eyes focus on each face,
May your soul take its imprint
Drawing each image within
As companions for the journey.
May you find for each one you love
A different locket of jewelled words
To be worn around the heart
To warm your absence.
May someone who knows and loves
The complex village of your heart
Be there to echo you back to yourself
And create a sure word-raft
To carry you to the further shore.

May your spirit feel
The surge of true delight
When the veil of the visible
Is raised, and you glimpse again
The living faces
Of departed family and friends.
May there be some beautiful surprise
Waiting for you inside death,
Something you never knew or felt,
Which with one simple touch
Absolves you of all loneliness and loss,
As you quicken within the embrace
For which your soul was eternally made.
May your heart be speechless
At the sight of the truth
Of all your belief had hoped,
Your heart breathless
In the light and lightness
Where each and every thing
Is at last its true self
Within that serene belonging
That dwells beside us
On the other side
Of what we see."

-John O'Donohue

Mona shivers after listening to this poem. "That touched my soul." She curls up next to Dru and lays on her lap.

Thoughts Of the Surviving Parent

Am I good enough? Am I funny enough? Do I make life fun like her dad did? I can't work on cars. I don't have as large of a network of friends and family in one state and one country. He was more of her hero. How do I become more like him? How do I make this up to my daughter? How can I be a father and a mother? Our lives have been flipped upside down. It is like when you are making pancakes and you mix the batter, and you toss the pancake up. Our pancake has come down and splattered into a million pieces. Andres is gone forever. Yes, Calley is a survivor and so am I, but why us?

I need Calley to go and do her annual medical checkups. She has always hated these. She only agreed to the checkups when she was in basketball because it was a requirement to play. The reality is most kids of color hate the medical stuff. I know it will be unlikely for her to get checked out. It is a battle I will not win.

I recently took CPR training and know that I can save a life. I also recently purchased a blood pressure cuff steaming from the result of Andre's death. He had high blood pressure. He had headaches. It was a brain aneurysm that took his life. I am thankful that Calley eats well and works out. I picture her lovely face in my head. Such an amazing soul that did not deserve this! Nothing to do but pick up the pieces; be grateful for the time she had with her dad and move on. It will be important to keep the memories alive and for her to visit Guyana and his house in Florida. I already know she will.

I am not crying. I am walking alone in my special quiet place. I am at a nature preserve in Florida where birds and animal life, trees and flowers are abundant. The heat beats down on you, but it feels good. There are many people of all ages and race that walk in the preserves. We nod at one another and say hello. Some stop to point out a type of bird, iguana, or alligator. I love this place and I always make time for it when in Florida.

Calley, Dakota, Thunder and Sundance have left for Montana. They had to go back to work. The new state and new surroundings will do Calley good. She loves to explore.

Brad is with his mom, Mona, and Dakota's parents at the campground. We will leave Florida later today.

I have many memories of when I lived here with Andres. The death of Andres and his mom happened so quick, in the blink of an eye. Andres's mom was old, and this was part of the cycle of life. Andres was middle-aged. Why was it his time to go and who decides this? Now I have a daughter who is in her twenties without her dad. How is this fair? Life is not fair, and I have learned this lesson a long time ago. I think it is an age thing. With age comes wisdom and with wisdom, knowledge. I hear a bird chirping and look at it. It is so beautiful, and I love the melodies it makes. And that's right, Andres was a huge animal lover like his daughter. He can no longer be out here to look at this wildlife. He can no longer work on his cars. He can no longer hang out with his friends or extended family in Florida and Guyana. His favorite beer sits untouched. His house and everything he worked for is still here, but he is gone forever... a life taken too soon! He was a person that meant so much to so many and is no longer here. The shock and horror of this revelation almost brings me to tears. The tears will not come right now. I must think my way through this. Perhaps later, I will take out my journal and write my way through this. I have to be there for my daughter, for Brad, for my friends and family. I have to become stronger and become better. I will never be Andres. I can only be me. Again, why did you take him and leave me? The question is not that I am ready to go because I am not. I want a lot more out of this life. I still have traveling, gardening, and writing to accomplish. Calley already was a child of two worlds, and she needed her dad. Damn it! I cannot fix this! I am frustrated. I am glad I am out here by myself. I stare at a family of Egrets as they walk by. I realize I am jealous that this bird family still has their dad. I watch the Egret family until they fly away from my view. I make a sound to clear my throat and I wipe my eyes which now have a mist in them. I walk in the direction that the Egrets flew but can no longer find this family.

I stare at a young boy in the preserve who is crying. His mom is speaking quietly to him "No Jorge, your dad is not coming. He was supposed to meet us here, but he did not show up again!" I think about the pain the mother and the little boy are feeling. I walk up to the little boy and give him the Egret feather I found on the trail. He smiles and for the first time today, I smile, and I nod at his mother. She nods back with a wisp of a smile and a quiet thank you that is expressed without words.

No One Knows What to Say When Someone Dies

Hope reflects on all the different things people have said to her and her family since the death of Andres.

The things that have helped her most are when someone hugs her, shares a memory of Andres, tells her they also have lost someone and can relate to the loss of a loved one. She realizes she hates when people say "I am so sorry to hear you lost someone. My prayers and thoughts are with you. Let me know if I can do any-thing." These words sting her.

Hope thinks about Calley and knows Calley hates it when people ask her a lot of questions about her dad. "What happened?" "How did he die so young?" All Calley knows is that he is gone, and nothing can bring him back. It does not help her to talk about it. It pains her. Although Calley loves to talk about her dad's love for cars, dogs, how he cared for his mom and also, the way he loved Calley. It helps her to remember who he was.

There are people who listen to your story and then say I will call you soon. Some call and some do not. Most people don't want to be bothered with death. And then there are the folks who say, "How are you?" Hope hates this question. Death is one of those things that you go through the stages which are shock, pain, anger, guilt, depression, and acceptance. The question of how you are is a difficult one due to these stages. Most of the time Hope finds this question triggers anger. She wonders in her head if it was her asking the other person the same question how they would feel after losing someone. She wants to yell "Do not ask me this question!" or "How would you feel is someone you loved died?" but has to hold back her emotions.

Everything is different when someone dies. You realize you will never see them again. You cannot pick up the phone and call them. As a parent, you will never share a story with them about your child again.

And then there is the child for whom the loss of a parent is a tragedy. The other piece of the parent whom she will never see again. The hugs she will never get, the trips she will never again take with this parent.

Hope also noticed Calley calls her less since Andres died. When he was alive, Hope heard from Calley every day. Now it is about three to four times a week. Hope can hear a deep sadness in Calley's voice that was not there before. She is too young to be sad. This too is a scar from the aftermath of death. Dakota has shared with Hope that when Calley sees a girl her age with her dad, she sheds tears. There was a day when they were on a hike and there was a father and daughter team hiking who smiled at Calley. Calley could not smile back and cried. The father and daughter team rushed to her side and asked her if she was ok. Dakota explained that Calley's response was "No, I will never be the same. I lost my dad." The pair was shocked as they knew Calley was young and said, "What happened?". To which Calley responded "I don't want to talk about it. "The pair walked away. Hope thinks of this scenario and realizes it is another example of how we do not know how to deal with death. The Nine Nights in Guyana was one of the best ways for Calley and Hope to cope. There were no questions, rather just a celebration of the person's life.

Hope has had to add melatonin to her sleep routine since Andres passed. She will wean herself off of this at some point, but the smell of death is too raw right now and she needs to sleep. Hope thinks about Calley who has told her since her dad passed, she can sleep but she wakes up and looks for him in the mornings or looks at her phone for a text or phone call that will never come. Calley holds Sundance and rubs her fingers on the collar that holds her dad's ashes also wishing for a miracle and nothing comes.

Calley and Dakota's co-workers have embraced them with love and kindness. One of their co-workers gave them both a big hug and then stood there and looked at them.

Calley explained to Hope how she asked the co-worker if she had something to say and she responded, "No, there are no right words when it comes to the death of a loved one." Calley hugged her and said thank you.

<h1 style="text-align:center">Memories of a Lifetime</h1>

Hope is in Calley's bedroom. She stores precious memories in this room. She opens a box containing trophies that Calley won while in basketball. She combs through the trophies and then opens another box which is filled with jerseys. She remembers the various teams, players, coaches, and other parents. She finds the box that contains the pictures of all of these people. So many memories! She finds a DVD and plays it. It is Calley giving a speech after a tournament. Hope takes in Calley's body, hair and facial expressions. She reflects on her age at the time of this video. She recalls being exhausted when attending all of the tournaments. Now she would do anything to have that much time with her daughter again; a time when things were different. Calley was younger and her dad was still alive.

Hope opens another box and looks through pictures of Calley and Andres. My God! When is the last time she looked at these pictures. It had to be twenty or more years ago. If he was still alive, she would not have opened this box. Life is so good and at the same time incredibly difficult. It is the loss of people, pets and relationships that mean something to us. The joys that we give thanks for become the losses we grieve. Grieving the ones we lost, not understanding why we lost them and questioning everything, and then questioning nothing.

There is no reason to fathom why the death of Calley's dad happened. Also, Grandma Iona died of a broken heart. *How could two people be gone so quickly?*

Hope wishes Calley were here with her. She knows she is with Dakota hiking in Montana. She wants to hold Calley, to stroke her hair, to stare at her beautiful face and tell her everything is ok. The problem is that nothing is ok, nor does it make sense. Calley is better off in the mountains with Dakota, Sundance, and Thunder. This is where Calley functions the best. It is her quiet place. Hope knows this is true for Dakota too. They both find peace when they are hiking.

Hope hears the song *Ain't no Mountain High Enough* playing in the kitchen. The smell of a tofu scramble permeates the air as Brad cooks in the kitchen. Sugar and Mountain come running into Calley's bedroom and jump on Hope. The pictures go flying. "Be careful girls. These pictures represent memories of a lifetime."

To Ease the Pain of Death?

Hope carries the vegetables from her garden and knocks on the door of a studio apartment. The young mom opens the door and smiles a smile of relief. Someone is coming to help her today. Justina has known Hope and her family since they moved into the farmhouse. Hope has been bringing the produce to Justina for two years.

"Hi Hope! Vegetables for me and my two little ones?"

"Of course Justina. Can I help you with anything else today?"

Justina smiles a sly smile and shakes her pretty black long, curly hair, "No, my two little ones are napping right now. Otherwise, they would come out and say hi. The produce really helps mi familia. Gracias Hope."

"De Nada Justina."

Hope heads to her car and drives to the soup kitchen. She is greeted by a tall lanky man with a face that has a look of completeness. "I am Maxwell and I run the soup kitchen. I am pleased to get another volunteer. What called you into the act of giving?"

Hope stares at Maxwell and takes in his dark brown eyes and his kind face. She feels safe with him and answers honestly, "I survived a death that I never thought I would live through. I must keep going for my family and for myself. When I help others, I feel fulfilled. It is the simple act of giving that provides me with completeness. When I look at your face, I feel like I see this look. Is this why you started the soup kitchen?"

Maxwell's face crumbles and he laughs uncontrollably. His laugh is deep and soulful. His pale skin is now red.

Hope is perplexed. "Maxwell, I had no right to ask this question."

"Hope, I did not anticipate your question which caused me to have an unpredictable response. No one has ever asked me this and I have been manager of this soup kitchen for ten years! I think I want to cry but my tears have long since stopped coming, which is why you get this uncontrolled laughter. I suppose it is better than crying. I lost my unborn child ten years ago. He was a stillborn baby."

"Maxwell, this must have had a profound impact on your life!"

"It did, my wife and I divorced and here I am. I find completeness in giving to others. I feel like I am doing something good for the world and making a difference."

"I have come to the right place. I want to make a difference too. Tell me, do you serve all types of folks, including folks of color?"

"Yes, my soup kitchen serves everyone. Why do you ask, Hope?"

"My daughter is a child of color and I need to make sure I am reaching out to everyone, but folks of color are especially important to me. Her dad was a person of color and he died unexpectedly at a young age. I don't know if I can ease my daughter's pain of death or my own, but I would like the opportunity to try."

"Please come in and I will show you around my soup kitchen. The rest of it is up to you. It is how you cope and how you handle the situation."

Home

Brad and Hope have returned home to their farmhouse and dogs.

"Brad, I am exhausted. Death is draining. I feel like I could sleep for a week. I miss everyone. It was good to see Andres's relatives. I loved Dakota's parents, and I don't think Calley could be with a better man than Dakota. Calley is sad but so strong. Montana will be a good place for them as it is a new adventure. We will have to visit them in Montana. We should take your mom and Mona when we go."

"That sounds like a plan Hope. I am glad to be home now."

Dru and Mona are at Dru's house.

Mona says, "Dru, Calley and Dakota are in Montana now."

Dru says, "How do you know, Mona?"

'Calley texted me and told me they had arrived. She is stunned by the beauty of my state."

"I am sure Brad and Hope will make a trip to Montana. We will go with them. Does this sound good?"

"It sounds perfect, Dru." "

"For now, Mona, I am just content to be home with my memories all around me."

Barb and Don are retired so home is wherever they make it. They are still on the campground in Florida. Santino has invited them to come over to have dinner tonight. The food smells delicious as they enter his home. He greets them with hugs.

"I made a vegan Caribbean bowl in honor of Calley. It is one of her favorite dishes."

"It smells incredible. Thank you for having us over. How do you like living in Andre's house?" asks Barb.

"I feel Andres and his mom's spirit within this house. I miss them both terribly, but I celebrate their lives."

"We were so sorry to see Calley lose two people she loved. We think she is an amazing girl and perfect for our son," says Don.

"I like Calley and Dakota together. I know her dad loved Dakota. Your son is going to help Cal survive the death of her dad," says Santino.

"Yes, he will," nods Barb and Don.

Calley and Dakota's job location has now changed from Arizona to a national park in Montana. They are both excited for the new adventure. Montana is a land of vast open prairies, glorious mountains, ranch towns and big blue skies.

"The land and the views are incredible here. I can see why Mona loves it," comments Calley.

"It is one of the most beautiful states that I have been," agrees Dakota.

"I am glad for a change of scenery. Now that my dad is gone, I really needed it."

Dakota says, "Yeah, you did Baby. How are you holding up?"

"I think about my dad every day. I cherish every moment I had with him. I miss him, but I am strong and must go on. I am so grateful for the people in my life, our dogs, the little things, like a vegan cheesecake slice after a long day."

"Calley, you are brave and the best woman I know. Hold your head up. I know how much your dad loved you and I only met him once. I am grateful I got to meet him. And you are right, you have a lot of people that love you. You can add my parents to that list. And girl, you already know I love you." Dakota leans over and kisses Calley on her full lips. Calley kisses him back. "Dakota, I love you too."

"This is the first time we have said this to one another. I knew I felt it but was scared to say it. Thanks for saying it back. I needed to hear that," says Dakota.

Sundance barks loudly. "We love you Sundance," says Calley.

"Dakota, I swear that Sundance understands the human language."

"Calley, I think she does."

"Should we take a hike on a new trail in beautiful Montana?" asks Calley.

"Yes, let's do it."

Dakota takes Thunder on the trail and Calley has Sundance. The views take their breath away as they familiarize themselves with Montana. As they are hiking, Sundance slips and falls. Calley grabs Sundance and falls to the ground. "Sundance, you cannot leave me! I have lost too much! She holds Sundance, grabs the collar with her dad's ashes and sobs. Dakota and Thunder stand behind Calley and hold her as she sobs. Dakota strokes her thick ponytail and rubs her back. Thunder curls up by Sundance and licks her face. No one says any words for an hour. Calley continues to sob. She looks at Dakota. "I have never cried like this. I am embarrassed."

"No Calley, it's good for you to show emotion. You miss your dad, and you are letting out some of your pain. You thought Sundance was going to fall, but you saved her. She is ok."

Calley's phone rings and she picks it up. "Hi mama. No, I am not ok, but I will be. Dakota, Sundance, and Thunder have my back. I miss my dad. I am grateful I have you and yes, I love you too. The mountains are calling me, and I have to go. I will find my strength and healing in these mountains."

Dakota says, "Calley, look what I found on the trail. Someone left it behind. I think they left it for someone else to find. It's a poem. Let me read it to you. Dakota takes Calley and scoops her up in his arms. He is cradling her like you would a small child. The poem reads:

"My lover lives in mountains killing my demons in his play. He brings me skull cups of sunsets to sip on at the end of the day. My lover hums a tribal song to put me fast to sleep. He pulls up a blanket of earth and tucks it around me."

—@whereintheworldpoetry.

"I like this poem, Dakota. Someone left it for us to find." Calley and Dakota gently kiss.

Sundance barks and Calley frees herself from Dakota's protective arms and proceeds to kiss Sundance and rub her collar, "Dad, I love you and I miss you. I always wanted to take you on a mountain hike. Remember we planned to do one in Guyana? Now you are here with me in spirit."

Dakota kisses Thunder. Thunder is getting tired, so he lifts her up and carries her as he and Calley continue their hike. They can hear the birds and are on the lookout for animals. There is a rush of excitement that runs through both of their bodies as they begin their journey in a new place. Calley is leading the way as always, Sundance follows, then Dakota and Thunder. Life is still good, but forever changed. They are in their happy place where they find peace, acceptance and set their own rules. It is a very comfortable place, and they welcome it. Calley looks back and smiles at Dakota. He grins back at her and nods, "Where are you leading us to Cal?".

"I don't know Dakota. I am exploring."

"It's ok Babe, I would follow you anywhere."

"I know this is true Dakota."

A light smile of gratitude forms across Calley's face for the first time since death turned her life into an unrecognizable journey.

When the Mountains Call You

The phone rings and Hope answers to hear her daughter's voice. Calley sounds strong and good.

"Mom, we are at the end of our hike for today. We hiked for four hours. The sunset is now behind us. We have reached our destination. Montana is more than I could have dreamed of. I know why Mona loves it. The nature, the mountains, the land takes your breath away."

"Where was your destination Calley?"

"That's the best part. We didn't have one. We still have another day before we start work. Our destination was whatever path we wanted."

"How did you know what the right path was?"

"That's just it mama, I had no clue, and I went with my gut. The path I chose turned out to be one of our best hikes ever."

"I guess the hiking paths mimic life in some ways, Cal."

"I was thinking the same thing, Mom. Sundance is taking good care of my dad's ashes. She licks her collar to keep it clean. She knows there is something very special on that collar."

"She has always been the smartest dog. I miss you Calley and I love you forever. Always remember this."

Hope places the phone down and joins Brad for breakfast. Brad looks at Hope. "Hope, are you here or somewhere else?"

"That's a good question Brad. I am here, but I am also somewhere else."

"Where are you, Hope?"

"I am where the mountains call you. I am where my daughter, Dakota, Sundance, and Thunder are. Will you join me?"

"Yes, Hope. I am ready to start a new chapter. I am ready to travel. We will live in an RV, but we can see Calley and Dakota more often. We have a lot of work ahead of us to make this dream a reality, but it is something we can do together. I too realized that life is short. I enjoy the mountains and they are calling me. The time has come to work on the next chapter of our lives."

Hope smiles a big smile and hugs Brad tightly. Mountain and Sugar come running into the room. They jump up and give kisses to all.

"No worries, Mountain and Sugar, you will come with us."

Hope calls Calley, "Cal, we will be selling our farmhouse, buying an RV, and traveling. This will make it easier to see you and Dakota. We will be near you. The mountains have called us, and we have also realized how precious life is and what we want out of it. How do you feel about this?"

"That's an easy answer, Mama, I lost my dad and I need my mom and my stepdad. To have you nearby would be good. Thank you for always loving me even though we are different shades."

"Calley, that was the easy part. I loved you for the shade you are. You have always been the most beautiful child to me because of the two worlds you come from. Always remember this."

Hope hears Sundance bark. "What did Sundance say?"

"Sundance is eager to have everyone nearby and she sends her love. One more thing mom, thank you for always having my back."

"It's been a pleasure Cal. See you soon."

Hope places the phone down and tears come down her cheeks. She stares out the window and cries. Her body shakes as she lets the tears trickle down. She plays her favorite song and continues to cry. Brad and the dogs are outside. It's ok. She needed this time to herself. These are tears of a lifetime and also tears for the life to come.